Pencil Art for the Beginner

Step By Step Guide to Drawing with Pencil

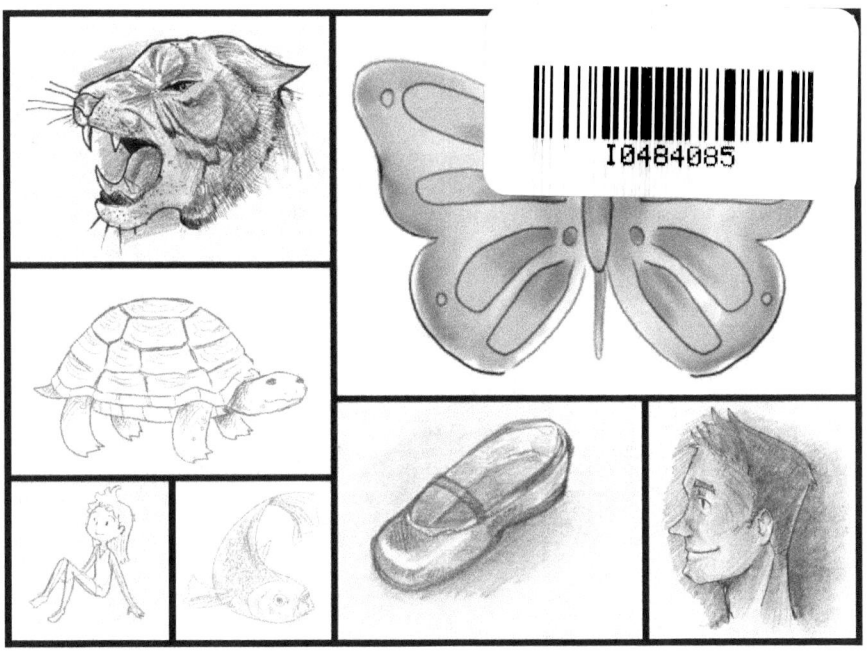

Learn to Draw Series

Harriet Kim Anh Rodis

Mendon Cottage Books

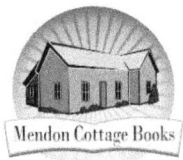

JD-Biz Publishing

Learn How to Draw Books for the Absolute Beginner

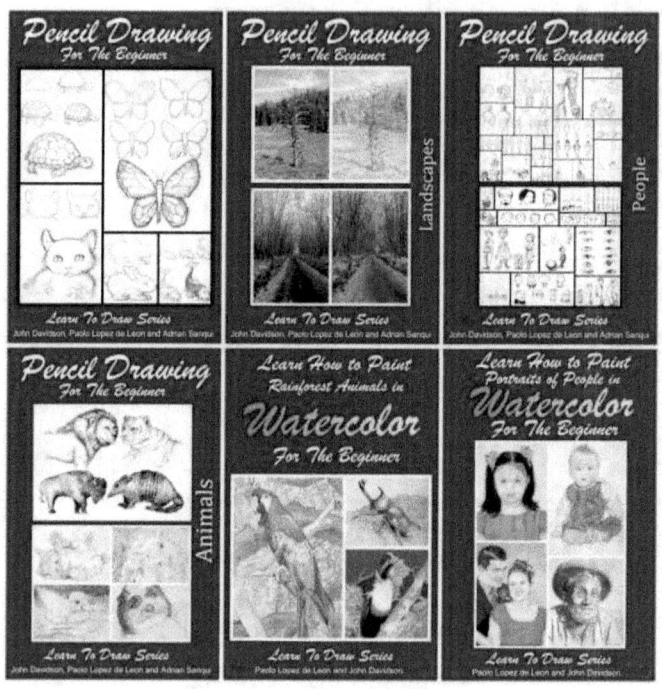

Our books are available at

1. Amazon.com
2. Barnes and Noble
3. Itunes
4. Kobo
5. Smashwords
6. Google Play Books

Table of Contents

Introduction

If you are an artist in search of further knowledge about drawing to enhance your skills, then this is not the book for you. This book is for the individuals who want to be an artist, but know nothing about drawing yet.

I know how it feels when you want to illustrate an idea but you just don't know how to start. You finally grab the confidence to mark that paper, but it turns out so terrible that you don't want to show it to anyone.

This instructional manual is for making that 'two circle' cat of yours into something more pleasing and distinguishable. It is also for enhancing that sheep which looks like a cloud with a face, and for turning your stick figures into cartoons, and more.

Read on to learn the very basics of drawing easily, by following this step-by-step tutorial. You can finally realize that drawing is something that is fun to do, and not something that becomes a cause of frustration.

Enjoy drawing!

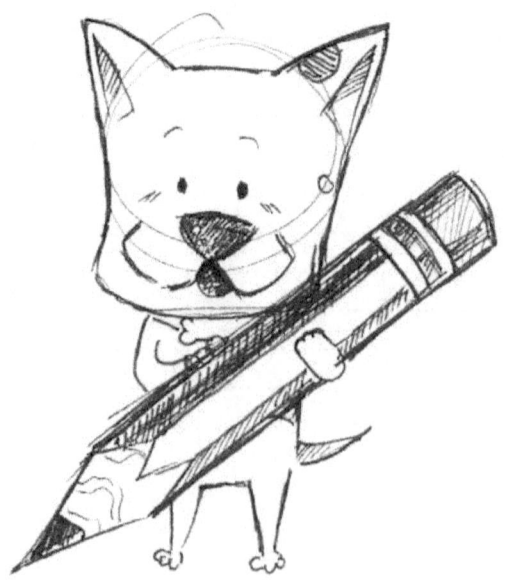

Getting Started

Drawing Issues

For starters, let us try to get rid of the few issues that make it harder for you to draw.

Stiff wrist

A stiff wrist is the reason why you can't make curved lines effectively. One common mistake of those who are just learning how to draw is that they move their whole arm to make a line stroke.

Hand's dead-weight

A hand with a dead-weight can only produce hard and thick line strokes. Sketches are composed of a lot of light and soft lines, so you need to lift your hands to modulate their weight and enable your wrist to move wider and more freely.

Drawing with elbow all the time

Drawing with your elbow does not literally mean drawing by the use of your elbow, but making strokes with a wide movement of elbows; even if you are just drawing a small image. You should relax this joint, because the main purpose of your elbow when drawing is to serve as a pivot. Also, to have the slight distance needed to avoid rubbing your hand against the paper. You need to gain more control over your hand strokes by moving your wrist and not your elbow most of the time, unless you are going to sketch on a large scale.

No idea how to start

This is normal to any artist, especially those who are just beginning. Just draw as if you know what you are doing. Give a little more effort and visualize your image, then try to capture it.

Drawing tools

Pencils

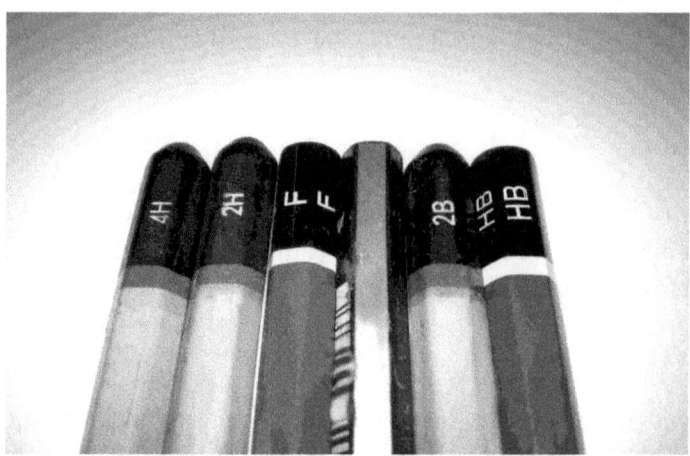

This is the most important tool, and is made from Graphite with a mixture of Clay. Soft pencils, like B, have a small amount of clay or none at all, and are used for outlining and giving texture to your drawing. They come in different scales: H (Hard), F, HB, and B (Soft) varying grades like 9H (lightest) to 9B (darkest) range.

For our drawings we need the following: 4H, 2H, F, HB, 2B and 6B, but if you're short of supplies, you can use HB only. Just apply pressure when you want a darker tone and light pressure for light tone.

Mechanical Pencils

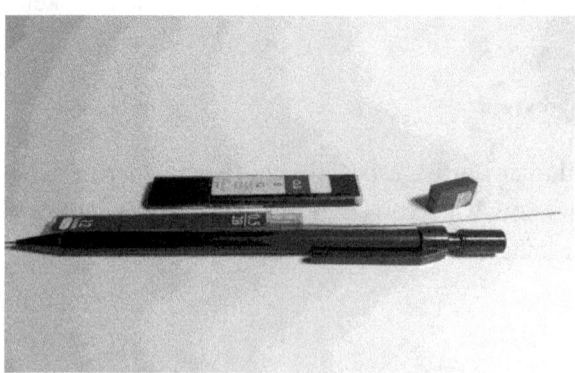

Like Pencils, the lead is also made of Graphite, and these are good for details. Mechanical pencils come in handy for tight areas. The main difference is that it doesn't need a sharpener if the lead breaks, you can just press the cap on the end of the pencil and it's good to go. They come in different sizes: 0.2mm to 5.6mm, but for our drawing, 0.5 will suffice.

Erasers

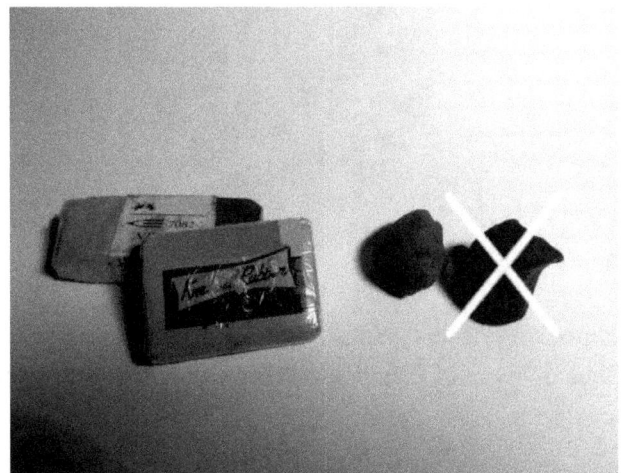

- **Kneaded Eraser**

This is like a clay or putty eraser, which can be molded into many different shapes and thicknesses. Depending to your needs, it can lift Graphite from the paper without any damage, it's good for tight areas, it can lighten areas in your drawing, and it is also used for making highlights in your drawings to make it more realistic. It will need to be replaced if it is already dark due to an accumulation of Graphite.

- **Vinyl Eraser**

This kind of eraser does not smudge the surface of the paper and it can erase hard and tough areas, especially large areas, and does not harden.

There are other types of Erasers like a Pink Eraser, Typewriter Erasers, and Peel-Off type Erasers, and you can also use those as it depends on the availability of the materials in your area. Feel free to experiment with what works best for you.

Sharpener

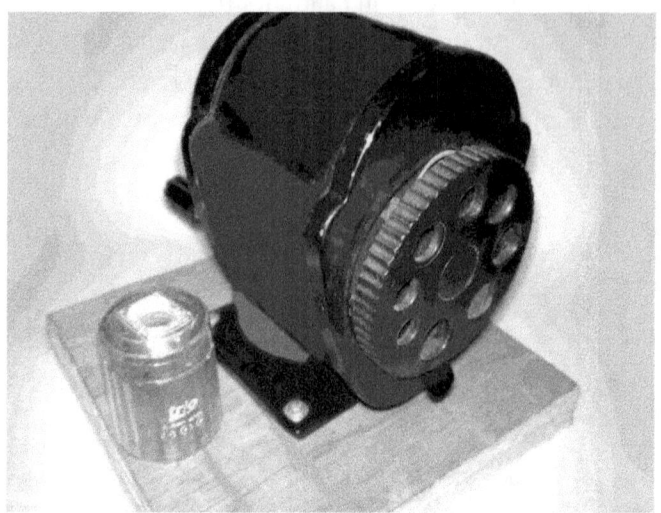

There are manual Sharpeners, Wall-Mounted Sharpeners and Electric Pencil Sharpeners, but any type of Pencil sharpener will do. Just make sure that it is safe to use.

Spray Fixative

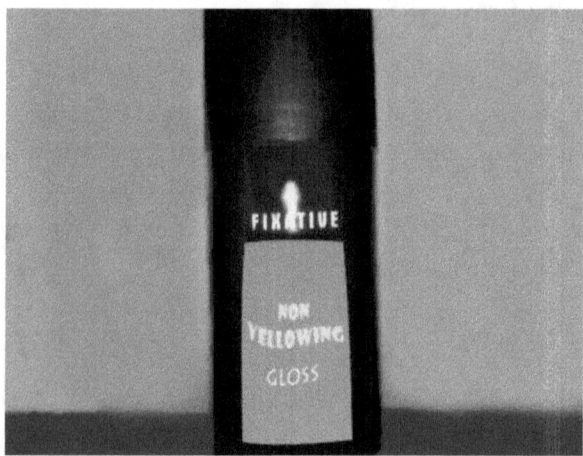

These are available in spray cans, and are used to make your drawing fix to the paper, so that it will not smudge and will have a professional look. They come in Matte or Gloss Finish, and it is better to choose a trusted brand and also one that is non-yellowing.

Smudge Sticks or Tortillon

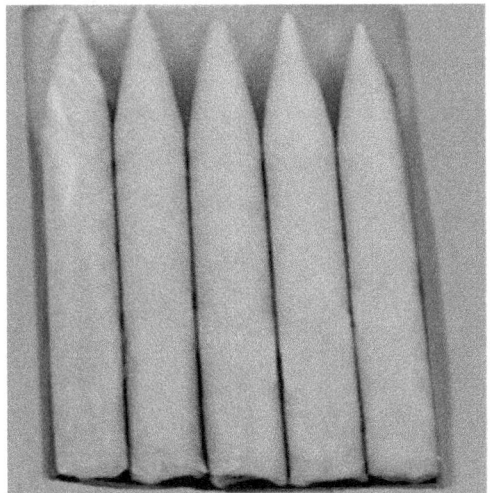

These are used to blend your drawing or smear one tone to another (this is the only time you are allowed to smear your work) when making even tones, especially in facial areas. You can use fine sand paper to polish the point when it's ruined, and when using one of these, position the tortillon at a 45° angle (Slanting "/") from your working paper.

Paper

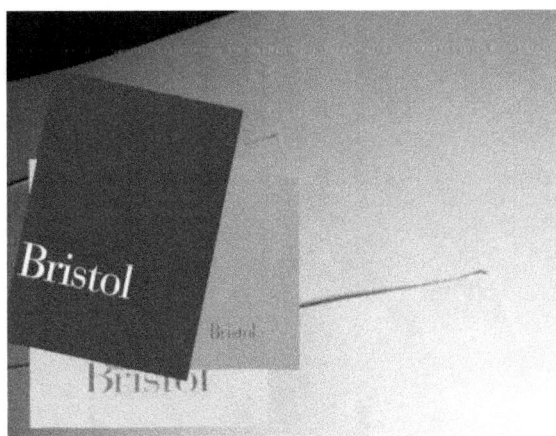

For our drawings, Bristol paper will be used. They come in boards and 2-ply pads, and the front has a Plate surface which is a smooth finish and has an egg shell texture. The back has the Vellum surface texture. I use the Vellum surface, which is good for shading. You can use other types of Vellum paper, but make sure it's the right one for drawing with pencil.

Ruler and Template

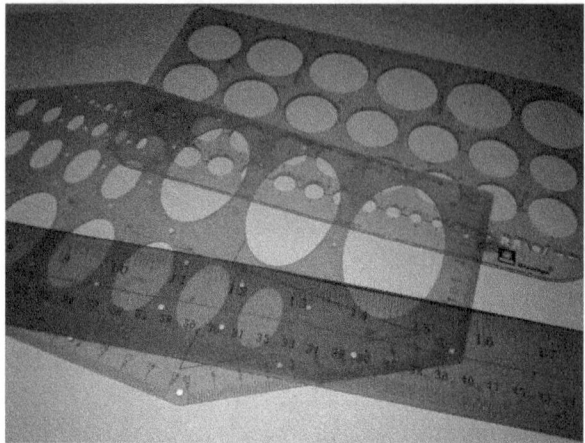

A Ruler helps you draw straight lines and measure distance. You can use a plastic or wooden ruler for our drawings.

Templates can be used to draw circles or ellipses accurately, especially when drawing the parts of the eyes, which demand a good form of shape.

How to grip a pencil properly

Writing grip or tripod grip - Using the point of the pencil

- Rest your pencil over your middle finger and hold it in place with your thumb. Then, put a light pressure on the pencil with your pointing finger.

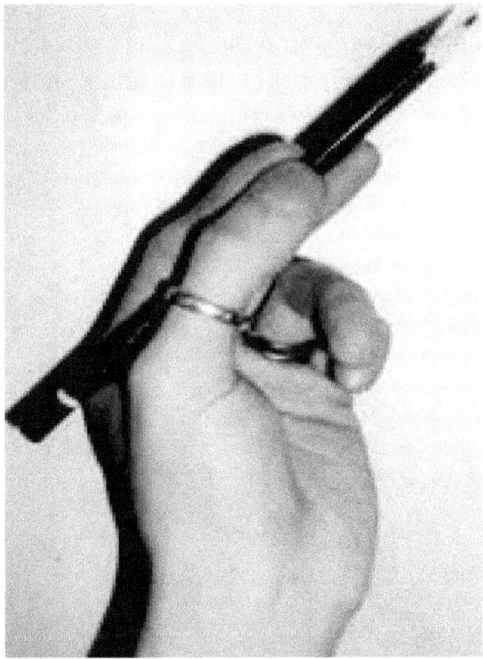

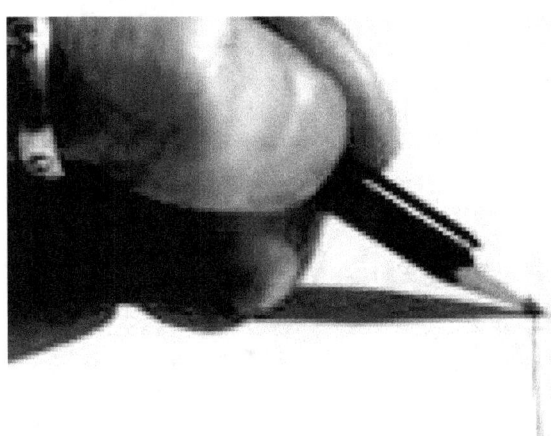

Benefit:

Since your hand is half-rested on the paper, you have **more control** on your line strokes, because the movement of your hand is very limited. This grip is most advisable if you need control over movement (drawing on a small scale, rendering small details).

Overhand grip - Using the side of the pencil

• Rest your pencil over your pointing finger and hold it in place with your thumb and middle finger (like holding a toothbrush).

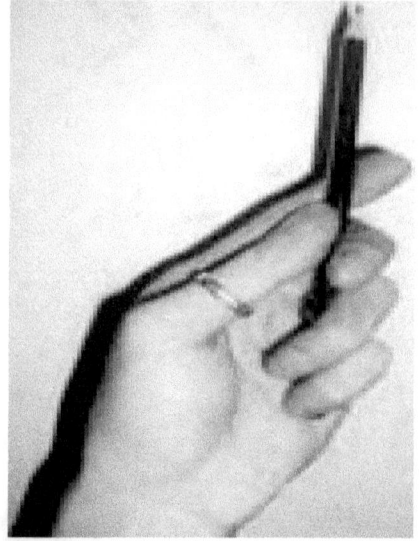

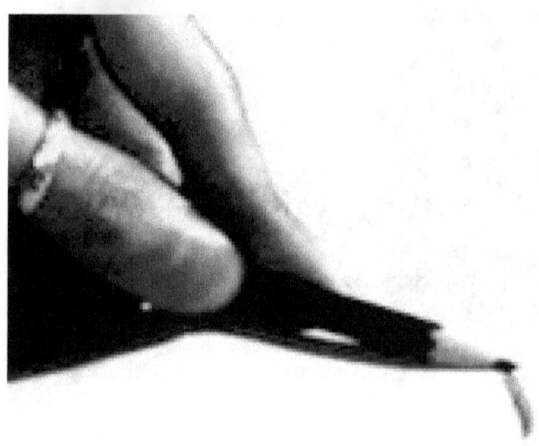

Loosely hold the pencil and apply controlled pressure on the side of the pencil's tip. This grip is often used when thick marks are needed (for shading) or for making a rough sketch that needs wide hand movements. Unlike the tripod grip in which most movements are done with the wrist and fingers, the overhand grip uses arm movements that mostly come from the elbow.

Gradually move your grip farther from the point of the pencil to widen your hand movement so you can make larger line strokes.

If your hand is not comfortable using the overhand grip, but you need thick lines, you can also achieve them with your writing grip adjusted up to the middle of your pencil, and leveling the side of your pencil's tip on the paper.

Benefit:

This is most advisable if you need movement over control (for shading and sketching).

Warming up

Warming up is important to get rid of your finger's stiffness and to work on the firmness of your lines.

Make repeated curves

Practice drawing circles repeatedly, by making a circle in a single hand stroke. It doesn't have to be perfectly shaped, and both ends do not need to meet.

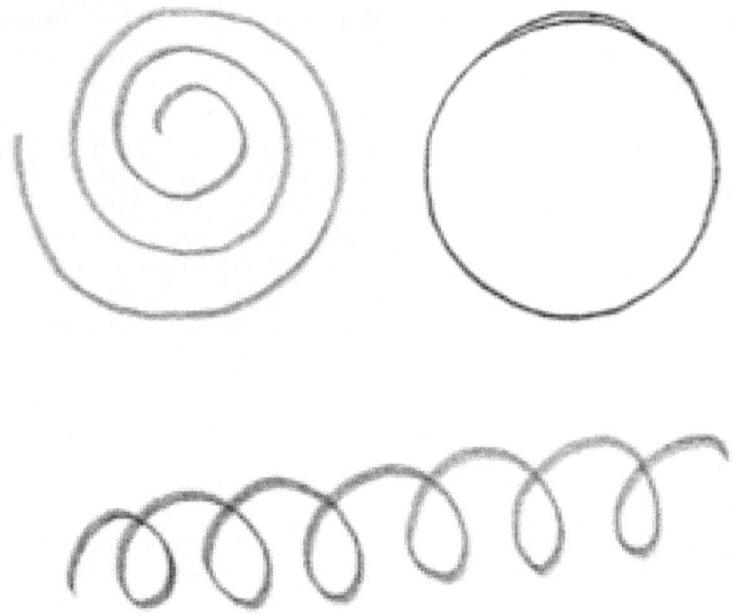

Draw straight lines

Work on the firmness of your lines. Draw straight lines with consistent thickness and length several times, until your hand remembers it and you can lessen unnecessary or accidental wiggles. Start by making thick lines, which are much easier. Draw at least 20 to 30 rows of thick parallel lines and then make the lines lighter and thinner to the point that they are barely visible.

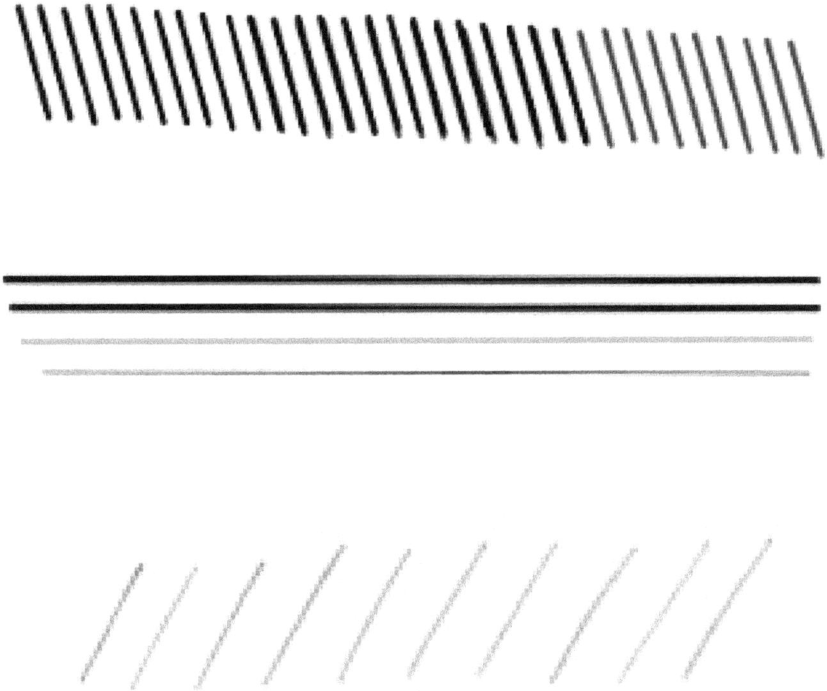

Basics -Elements of Drawing

These are the basic and fundamental elements of drawing.

Dot/ Point

•

Lines

A line is defined as a series of connecter points that extend from one point to another, wherein the edges of the line don't meet.

1)   Straight line

Straight lines are lines that don't curve. They can be horizontal, vertical, or diagonal.

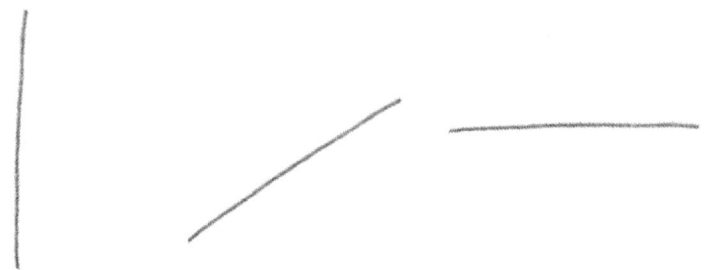

2)   Curved line

Curved lines are lines that have curves or gradual changes of direction like as shown below.

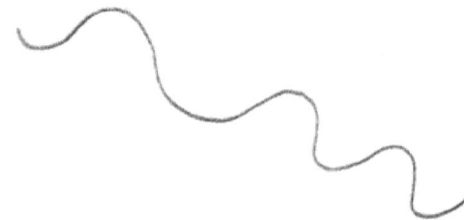

3) Zigzag line

Zigzag lines are lines that form edges as they changes direction.

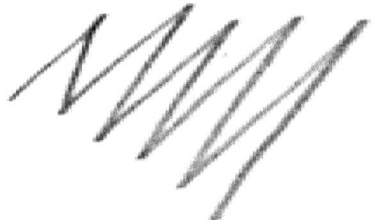

Shapes

Circles

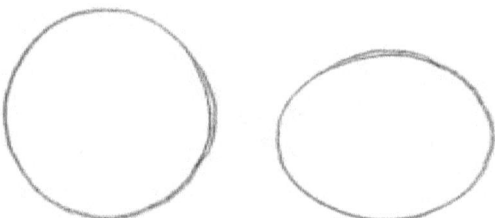

This is a shape that doesn't have any edges. It can vary in length and width and can be oblong.

Triangle

This is a shape that has 3 edges.

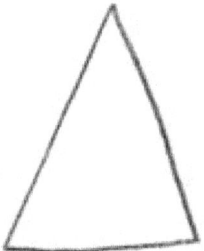

Polygon

These are shapes with "many edges" as the name implies. It includes squares, trapezoids, and other shapes with many edges.

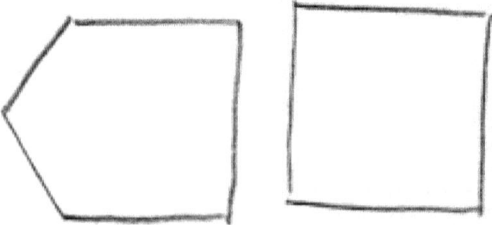

Usual Errors

Drawing how you see it rather than what it really looks like

When most people draw, they just draw how they imagine it to be, not how it really looks. Like the figure below, most people may draw the leaf to look like the leaf on the left, disregarding the crinkles, the width of leaf, and other details. Compare it to the one on the right, which shows the details of the actual leaf.

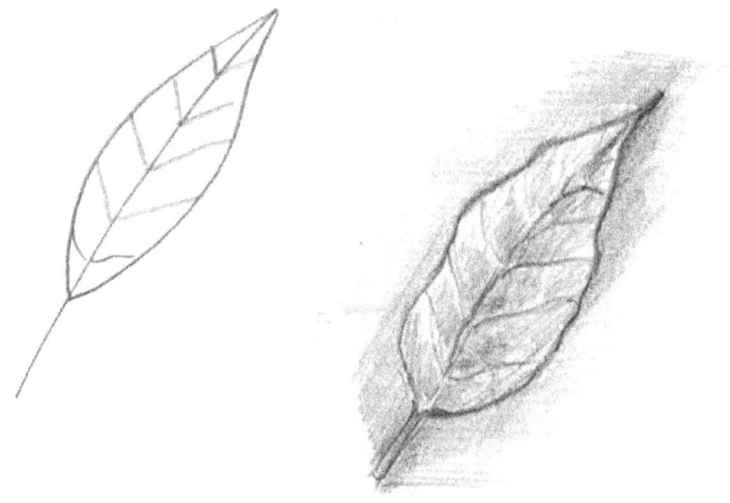

Another example is the typical drawing of a cup, shown below. You can see that since the surface is perceived as flat, the base of the cup was drawn as a horizontal line rather than curved line.

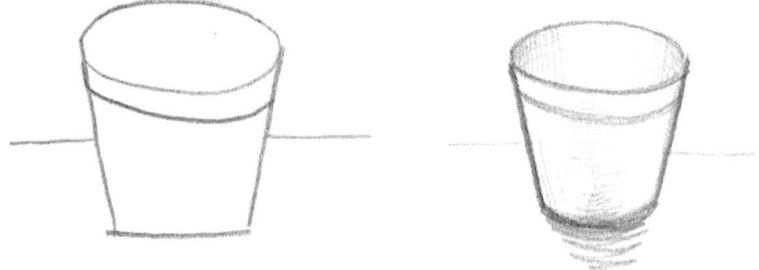

Perspectives

Perspective is basically a point of view. It is the art of drawing solid objects on a two-dimensional surface to give the right impression of their height, width, depth, and position, in relation to each other, when viewed from a particular point.

2-point perspective

Here we see a horizontal line with 2 points near the edge of the line. These 2 dots are the **banishing points** and the horizontal line is our **horizon.** The further the object or the part of the object is, the smaller it seems to be.

When drawing with perspective, make an initial sketch of lines from the banishing point to the position of where you want the object to be.

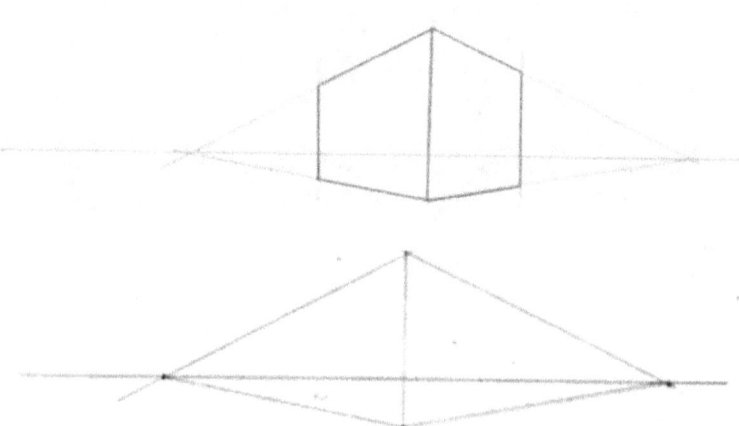

Then draw the object using the lines that you made as a guide.

Rule of Thirds

Another golden principle of drawing and design is the rule of thirds. This is where the image can be divided into 3 by 3 equal parts and the elements are placed along the lines or their intersection.

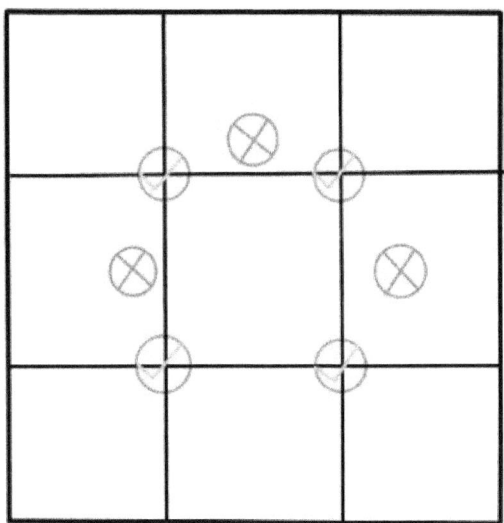

In the figure above, we see the parts where the elements are recommended to be placed (where green circles are located) and not to be placed (where the red circles are).

Below are examples of using the rule of thirds (1) and not using the rule of thirds (2).

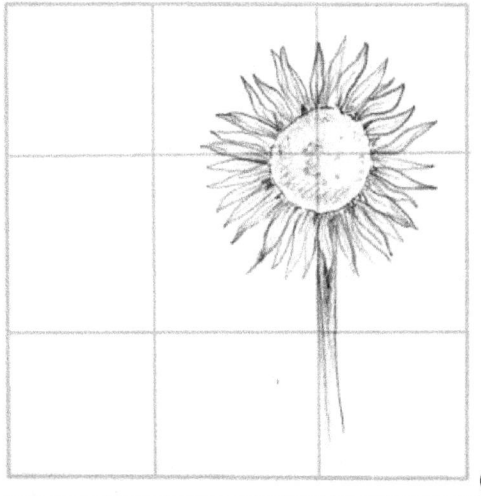

(1)

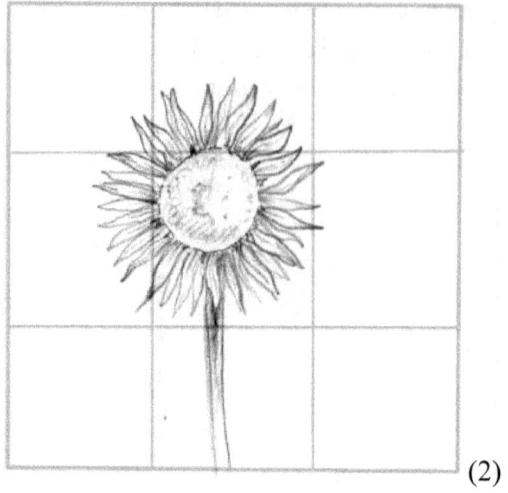

(2)

Drawing

Overview of making a pencil art

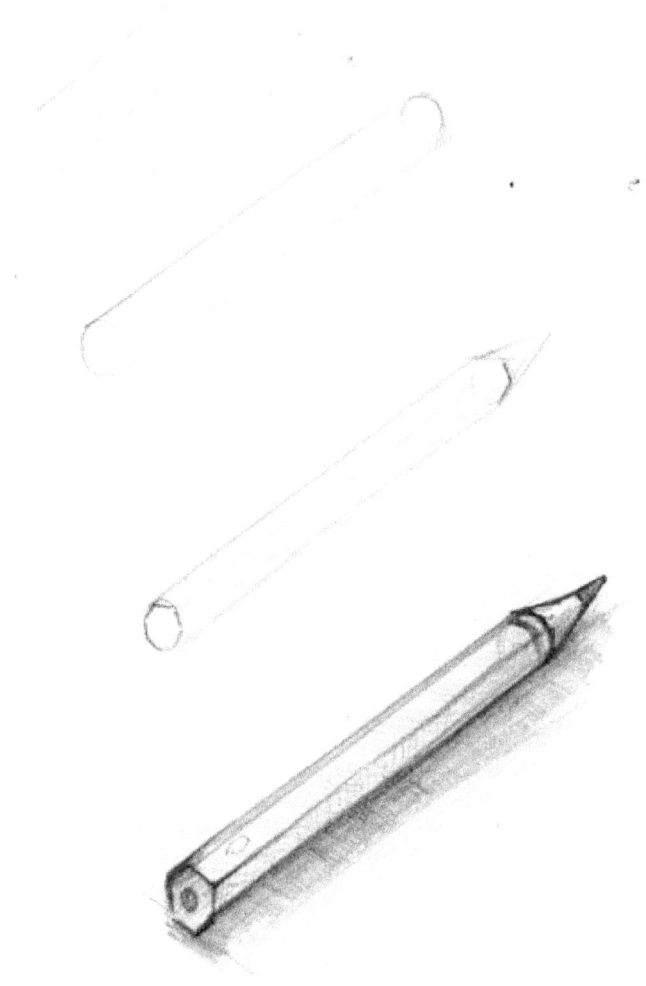

Start with the basics

A primary sketch is just your initial sketch. Start first with basic lines and shapes. Here the artist started by drawing 2 parallel lines.

Add the shapes /silhouettes which are the main outline of your drawing as a whole. This can be a combination of basic shapes such as boxes and circles which will represent the mass of the object/subject you are going to draw. In this drawing, the artist added 2 circles at both ends to make a tube like outline. Then, the shape of the pencil tip was also added and the texture of the pencil shaft.

Define permanent outlines

Trace your sketch to clearly define the primary details or suggestive contour. These are the particular parts that are necessary to convey your subject's basic form in your drawing and make it easily perceivable. These are essential parts such as the ears, eyes, and nose for a head. Some drawings cannot be distinguished easily because they lack suggestive contour lines, especially when conveying a subject's dimension value.

Clean it up by erasing the sketch markings.

Show/illustrate some texture

Texture contour provides a better portrayal of the shape's dimension values. The details such as scales, fur, or any print and texture should curve and flow with the contour shape of your subject, so adjust it accordingly.

Add some shading (light impression). This is the representation of your drawing's light and dark values. Applying shades will give your object/subject the visual depth it needs to define the proper volume or proportion of your shape by verifying its angle via dark and light tones in harmony to your preferred point of light.

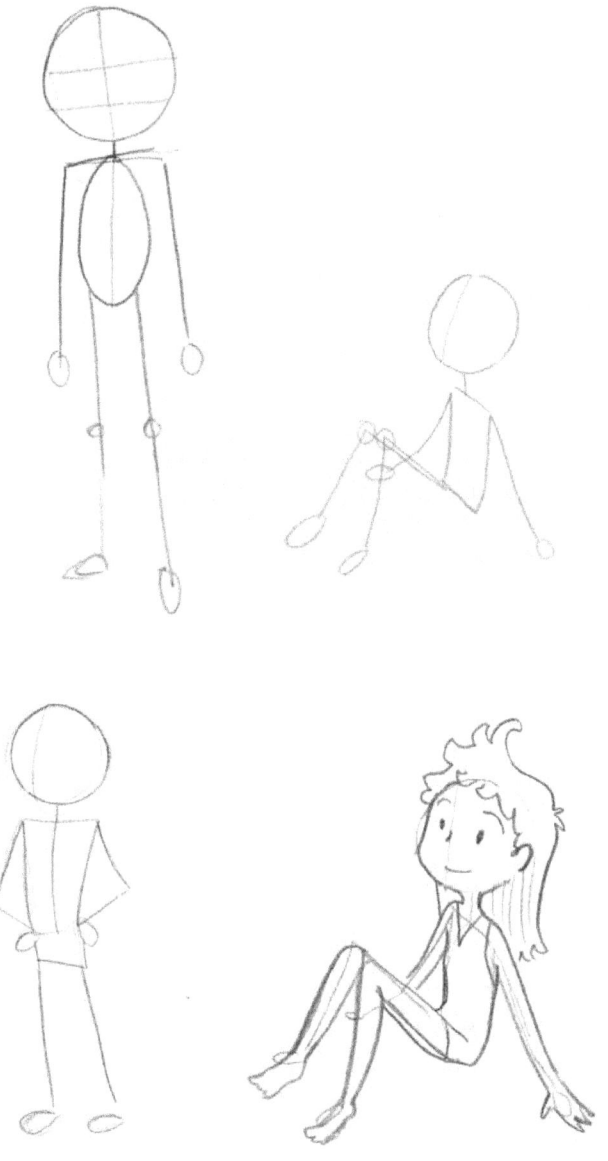

In sketching, starting with basic shapes is important. For example, when drawing a cartoon person, it may look hard, but if you start out with the initial sketch, it will definitely help.

Rendering

Rendering is the process of formulating, adding color, shading, and texturing an image. It is important to make your drawing have more life and effects.

Each kind of pencil ranging from 9B to 9H has different tones. Tones are light and dark values. The softer the pencil is, the darker the tone it will produce.

This is our **value scale** and this will help us select the right tone.

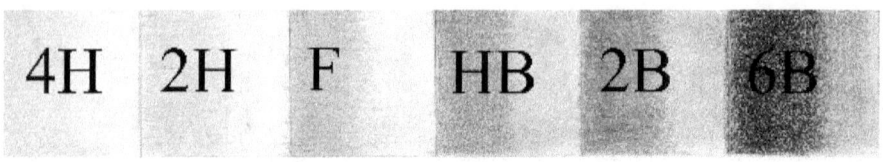

You can make your own Value Scale to have a reference, take note that I blend (using the smudge stick) to the right, so that you will have an idea, how will it look like.

Shading

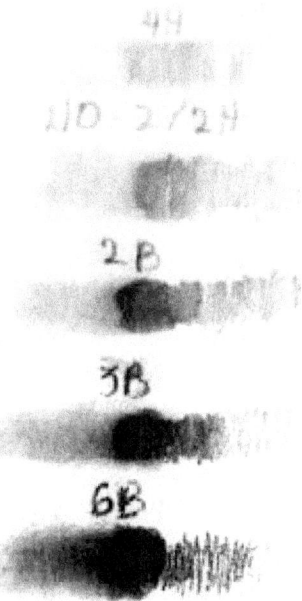

Shading is used to portray the light and dark values of an object or any subject by applying gradations accordingly (to the contour shape). You do this via controlled line weights, number of lines per set, and the manner of how it should travel across the subject, which enforces the illusion of your subject's three-dimensional appeal.

If your subject does not have any kind of designs, embellishing details, or anything that may portray the dimension values of its shape, use shading to convey its three dimensional form effectively.

Drawing tools matter the most in shading. You are probably using a 2H pencil because that is the most common kind that you can buy anywhere. But, if you are going to shade with this pencil then the deepest shade you can produce is silver, no matter how much pressure you put on it.

H stands for hard, so the higher the number, the harder and lighter the lead becomes.

B stands for black, so the higher the number, the darker and softer it gets.

There are pencils that are labeled as HB and this means that the lead is hard but it can produce a dark tone. If you are going to smudge your shading then you should go for a "B pencil".

Kinds of Shading

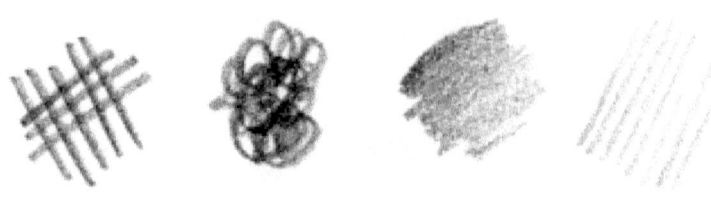

Hatching

Hatching is the simplest way of initiating linear shading (shading via lines).

To apply hatching, make parallel lines, to the portions that should be grayish, with thin and light sets of lines (not the farthest portion to have the darkest tone, and not the nearest portion which should be left as is).

To obtain dark shades, re-shade the portion with another set of lines in the same direction, or use a thicker set of lines, as shown in the figure above.

The idea is to control the visibility of the paper's whiteness by covering it with analogous lines in order to produce a grayish appearance. You can also totally hide it by making the lines closer to each other to achieve a dark tone rather than making thicker lines or applying another set of lines, which can only be done with graphite or charcoal pencils.

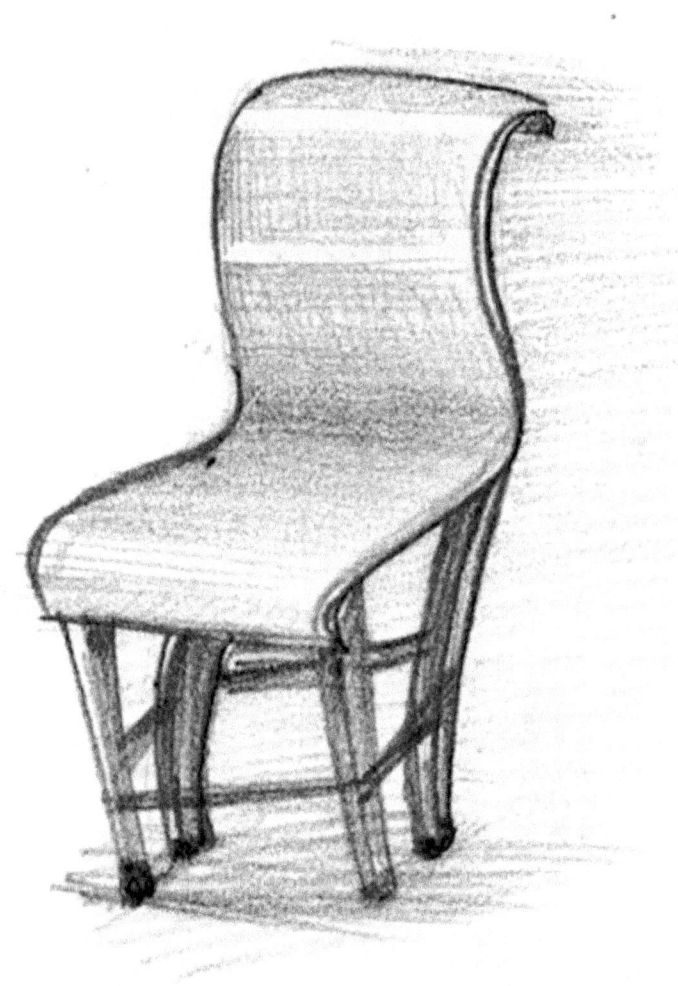

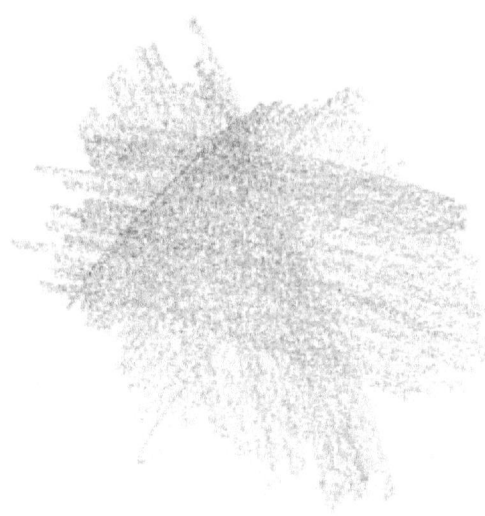

Cross-hatching

Cross hatching is the same as hatching, but this time you will oppose your first set of lines by overlapping it with another set of lines, in a different direction, to form a grid.

Increase the dark tone by overlapping line sets coming from different directions, until you reach the depth of tone you desire.

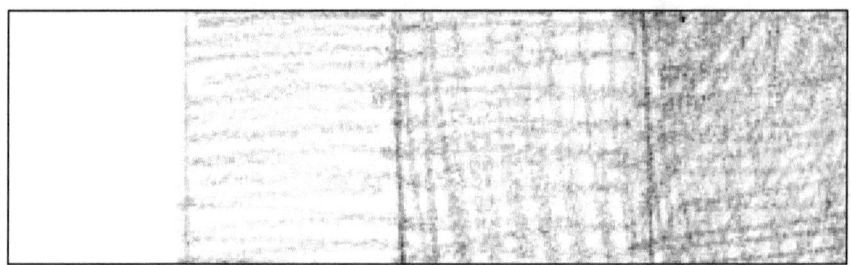

When using both of these methods, you should always take note of your subject's dimension value; the lines should bend according to the subject's contour form. The line sets may break and leave a gap to convey the subject's realistic nature aside from the line thickness and the number of line sets you use to regulate the tone. Linear shadings should portray or depict how your subjects occupy space, and this is what artists call **Cross-contour**.

Cross contour are the lines that travel across the subject's basic (contour) structure to convey its (three-dimensional) contour form.

- A fold in a fabric, visible ridges, or any kind of minimal or noticeable change on the surface of the subject can be described or emphasized by cross-contour lines.

- Start with a slanting set of lines and try not to use perfectly vertical or diagonal lines.

- Subjects with perfectly straight hatches tend to look flat especially if it will not be overlapped by another line set.

- You can use vertical or diagonal lines if your subject is already tilted or angled or if you intend the subject to look flat such as even planes and non-dimensional buildings.

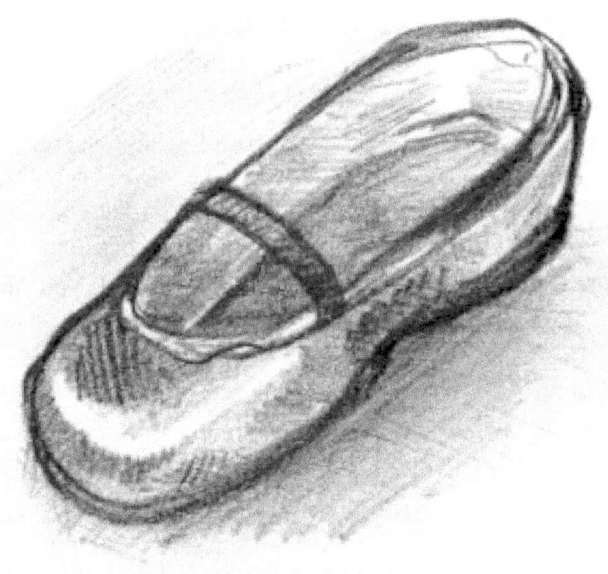

Scumbling

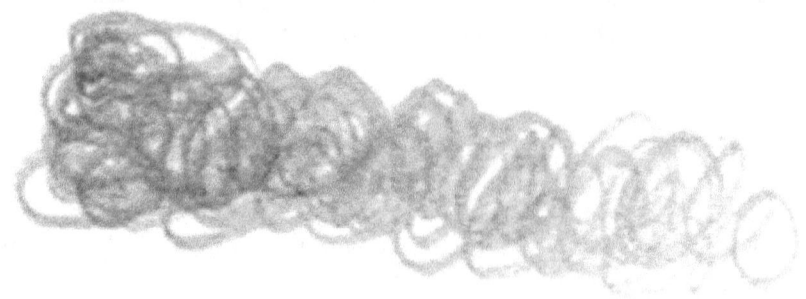

Scumbling is an effective way for shading without much precision needed such as harmonizing the bending of lines to the contour shape. Unlike hatching, which modulates the tone by adjusting the exposure of the paper's whiteness by the number of line sets and line thickness, you will adjust the tone by circling lines or infinity-shaped markings.

Apply the shades by making small, nearly freeform, scribbles with circling marks. Because you are simply making scribbles, you will naturally leave some small spots unmarked, which is the same idea with the little spaces between the lines when you use hatching. The toning depends on the pressure you put on your lines or by the number of times you get back on the same portion of the subject.

Scumbling is often used as a preparation for smudging because the marks you are leaving are essentially loosely synced on the paper. If you smudge it, the scribbled marks will easily lose their form and appear as a single solid tone or a faded shade.

- Use a fine point pencil if you don't intend to smudge or smear it later on, as this will effectively produce scribbles with consistent size or thickness.

- Scumbling can easily produce a texture that is relatively comparable to a brillo pad.

- Use a blunt point pencil and/or the side of the pencil if you want to produce thicker scribbles which are most effective if you are going to smudge or smear them afterwards.

Stippling

Stippling is a shading method in which you will use dots instead of lines. Although, using this technique is not quite typical for starters because it takes a lot of time to finish. For those who lack control in shade tones (getting too dark or too light), this is an effective approach to gain control of modulating proper shade values.

The depth or lightness of the shade is modulated by the distance between each dot you make, like portraying the light and dark values of a subject via grains. It is the same as hatching and scumbling (adjusting or limiting the exposure of the paper's whiteness), as the tone will appear lighter as the gap between each dot increases, and darker as you draw them closer and closer to each other.

- For starters, practice using this method by marking or remembering the portions of your subject where the shades suddenly change their tone, and establish it by making the dots relatively aligned or organized.

- Stippling can easily produce a texture that is closely similar to sand paper, which is very useful for subjects that should have a rough quality or appearance.

What separates the dots as 'textures' and the dots as 'shades' is the size of the dots, the pressure you put when making it, and most especially, the manner of how they are placed.

- Use thicker dots when establishing shadows.

- Mark dots in random to portray a texture.

- Align the dots (like hatches in cross-contour) for establishing shade values of the subject.

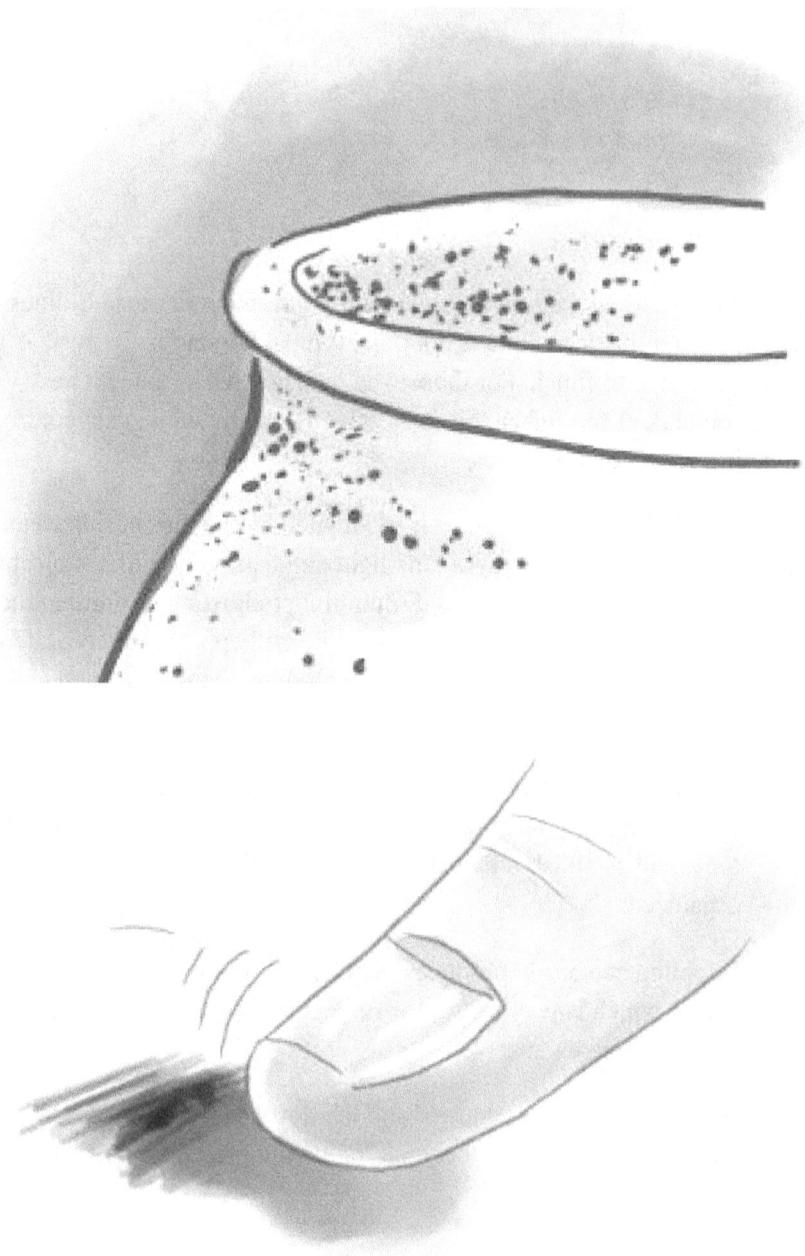

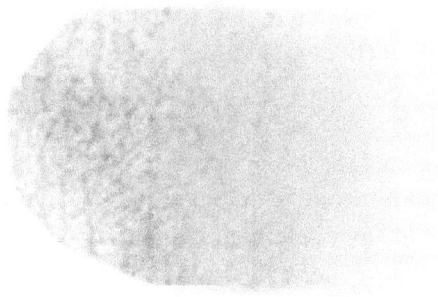

Smudging

To smudge is to flatten out a given shade by smearing your primary shading by pressing it against the paper evenly. You can try it with your own finger, a piece of cloth, or just a small piece of paper. I wouldn't personally suggest these methods if you are drawing seriously, because a cloth has a natural texture that leaves a pattern and might just damage your shading. Also, your fingers have natural oil that would be absorbed by the paper and it will ruin the shading.

Artists use tortillion (a paper rolled in a tight cone-shaped figure to make a pointy wick) or a smudge stick/blending stump for smearing shades, especially in hard to reach portions such as eyes, earlobes, hair strands, etc. You can use a kneaded eraser (an eraser that can be molded or formed easily like clay) for making thin highlights.

As an individual who knows nothing about drawing, you might ask yourself if these tools are really necessary. Well, the answer is yes. But, if you really don't want to spend a penny on buying a blending stump or kneaded eraser then just simply make your own tortillion with a thick piece of paper, so you can at least know or experience the advantages of having at least one of these tools. You can use a cotton ball for smearing large portions.

Smudging your drawing will basically blur the lines you made earlier. The certain line strokes, especially those that are loosely fixed on the paper (light line stokes and scribbles), will merge with the other lines, making it edgeless.

This technique is used to soften the texture and make the different shade values work as a single piece. Smudging will make the shifting of tones blend with each other effectively, but the strong line strokes or the lines made with great pressure will not be blurred completely, or it may not even be smeared at all.

- Smudge the portion you want to blur in a circular motion, don't just rapidly stroke in any random direction or you might create an unwanted mark or pattern.

- Stroke outwards to make thin diminishing line marks for making hair strands, gray toned highlights, or anything comparative. With a pressure stressed from the starting point, decrease it as you end the marking (signatory line strokes), starting from the segment where the graphite marks are originally located.

- Rub your blending stump or anything you are using for smudging with a controlled pressure. Too much pressure will scratch the paper and it will catch the excess graphite which will leave an inerasable stain.

Rendering an object doesn't limit you to using only one kind of shading. It can be a combination of two or more shading kinds, and an example would be this drawing:

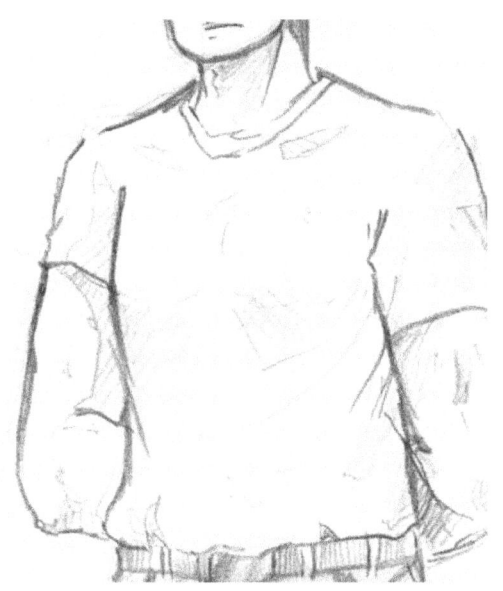

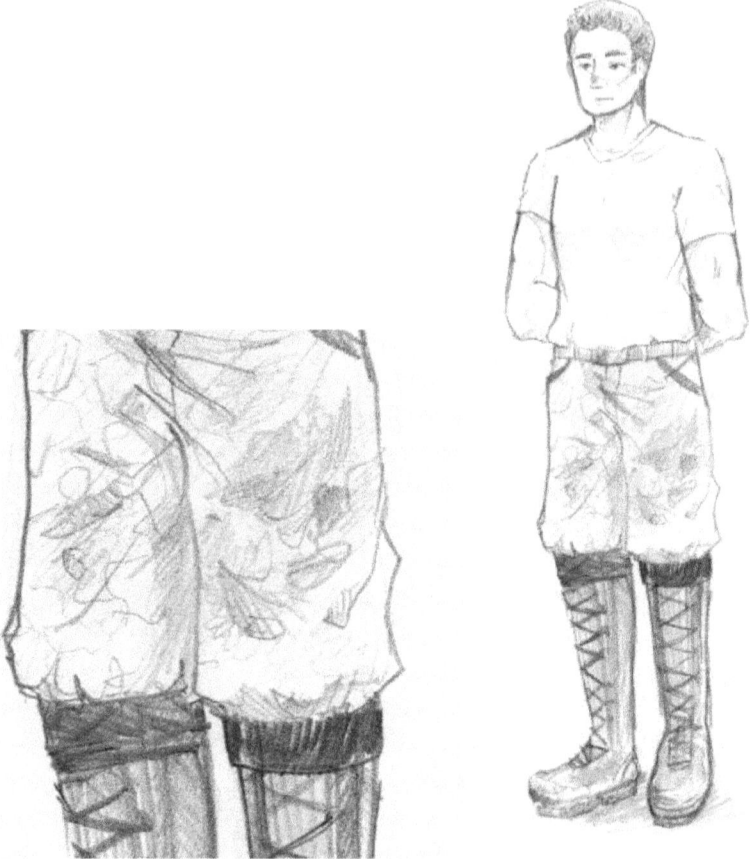

Here you can see the combination of hatching, cross hatching, scumbling and smudging.

Casting shadows

Lighting

One important thing to note, before starting to shade, is the direction of light. In the drawing below, observe how the lighting can affect the object.

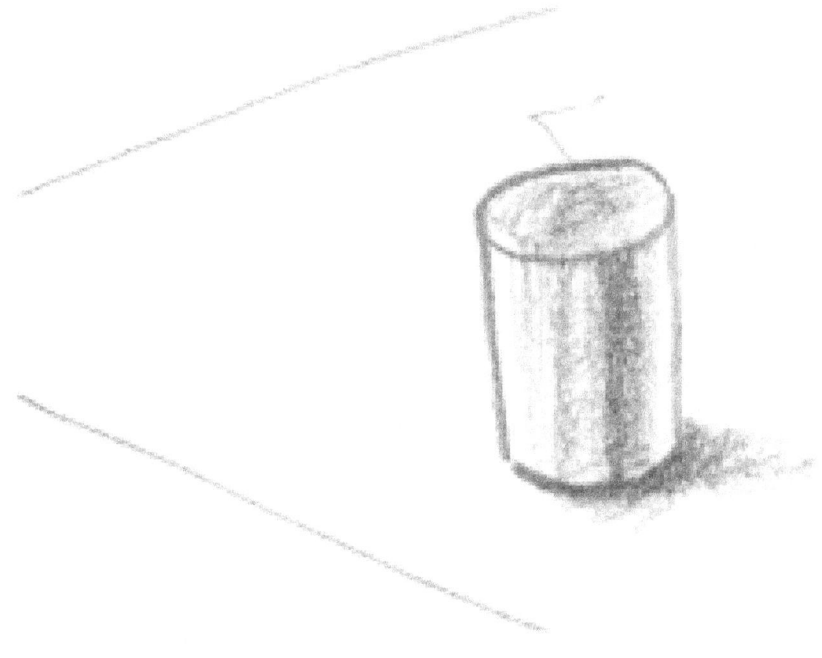

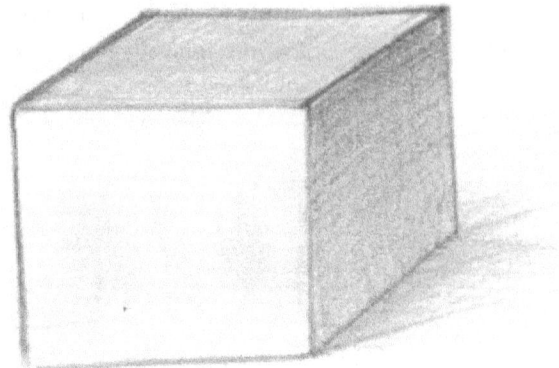

To easily figure out where to place the shadows, cast it on the opposite side of the brightest tone your subject has.

Also, the farther your drawing is from the paper (visually), the bigger and lighter the shadow becomes, and vice-versa.

- For drawing illustrations that consist of more than one figure, the shadows should also bend accordingly to the dimensions of the portrayed plane or background.

- Re-outline the shape and darken the sides carefully including the shadow.

The dark shades under the petals convey the light coming from above. And the equally distributed gray tone inside the main outline initiated with hatches portrays the evenly flat surface.

Sphere

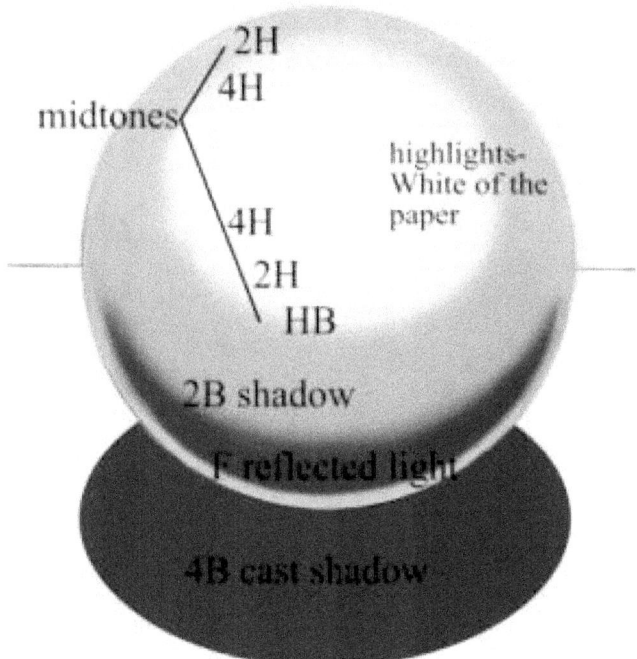

Above is our guide of what pencil to use to get the following tones of an object. The light source is coming from above.

4B – Cast shadow; the shadow cast by the object, depending on the placement or location of light. It's the place where no presence of light can be seen.

1F or 2F - Reflected light

Kneaded eraser and white of the paper – Highlights

2B – Shadow; it is where the light source cannot reach, and is always opposite of the light source.

HB, 2H and 4H – Midtones; It's the place where the transition of light is evidently present, that is why we will be using different grades of pencils for this. Our orientation for this is from dark to light when rendering.

Highlights - This is the part that we're going to use the white of the paper or a kneaded eraser if there is a presence of tone from shading.

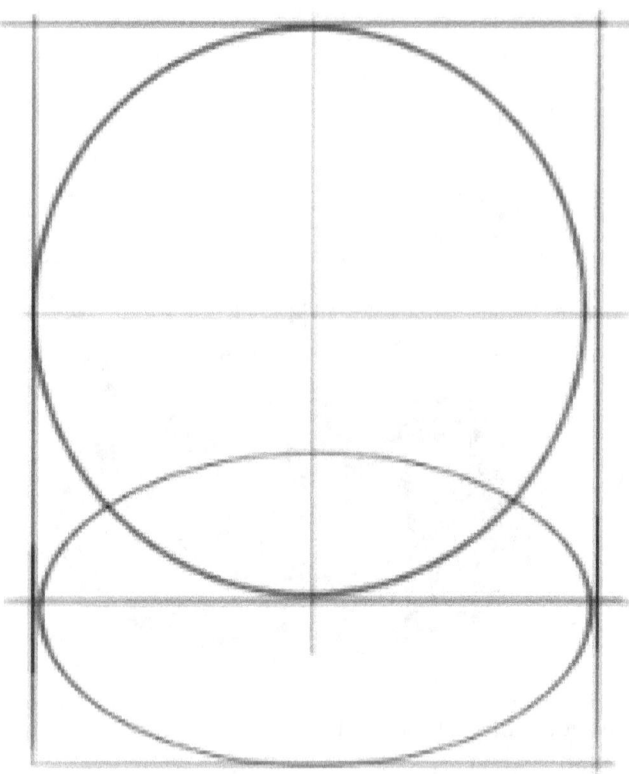

Step 1. Draw a circle using your 4H or 2H pencil or use your circle template. For the cast shadow, use your ellipse template and draw a line in the middle of the circle, as this will be the table.

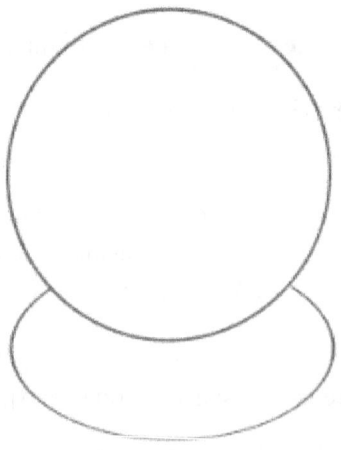

Step2. Erase the unnecessary lines.

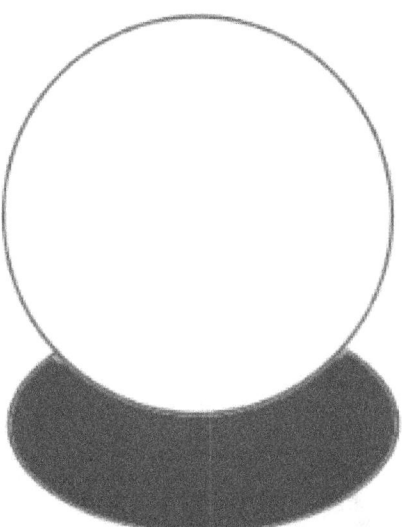

Step3. Let's start rendering the cast shadow using 4B, as this is the darkest part of our drawing. Remember that we are going to render this from dark to light, building the pencil lines gradually up and down, matching the value of our example. Then, blend the cast shadow using your smudge stick. It is better if you only use this smudge stick for this tone.

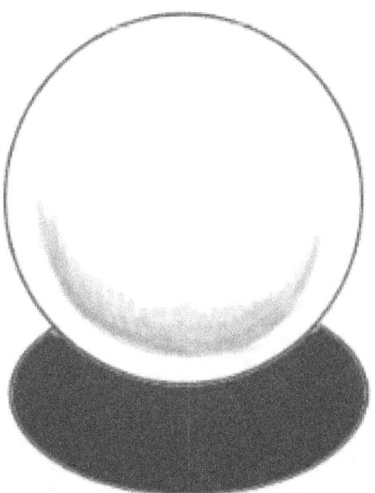

Step 4. Using your 2B pencil, we're going to draw the shadow. Do shading strokes around the ball and remember to leave some space below it for our reflected light.

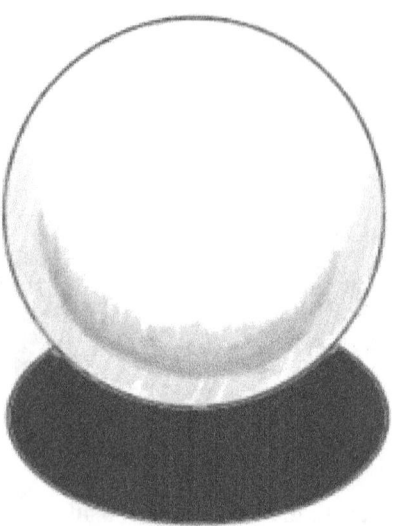

Step 5. Next is the reflected light. Use F pencil, and apply shading strokes below the shadow, the same as you did in Step4.

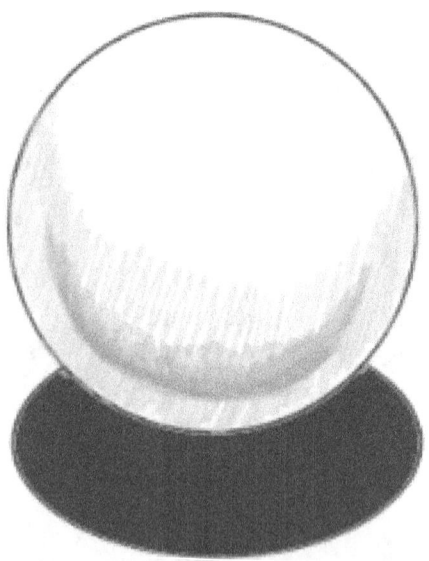

Step 6. Working with our Midtones, we will be using HB, 2H and 4H. Starting with HB, apply strokes above the shadow.

Then with 2H, apply strokes above the HB stroke, and also apply light strokes in the upper part of the inner circle.

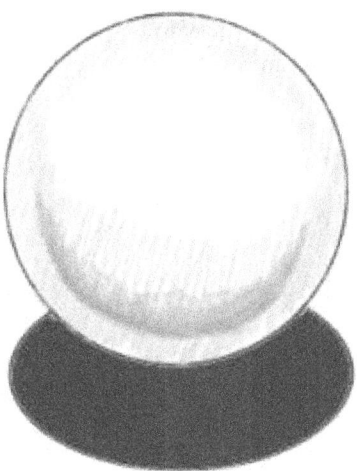

Do the same using 4H, just above the 2H, and also apply light strokes below the 2H.

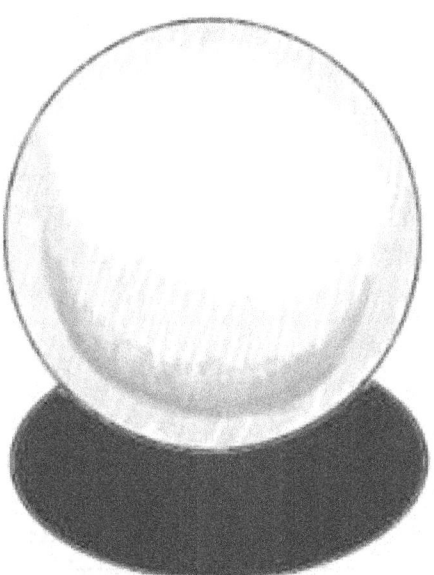

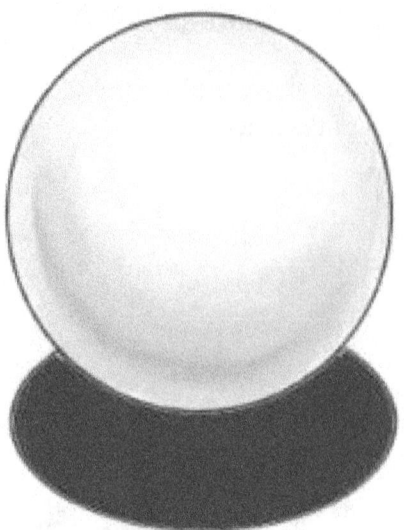

Step 7. It's time to Blend these tones, so we will be working from light to dark. Be sure to clean your smudge stick first, as there must be no graphite to it, so not to darken any of our light tones. A new one would be better or just use sand paper to polish it.

Starting at the upper part, blend the 4H tone (going upward then downward) to the 2H tone, and your stroke will be the same as when using pencil.

Do the same with the rest. Start blending from the 4H tone to 2H then HB, slowly and gradually. For the shadow with 2B tone, lightly blend it upward to HB. For the F tone (reflected light) blend it starting from the left side going circular to the right side, and be sure not to have contact with the 2B tone. After that, clean your work using your eraser.

Tips:

- If you accidentally blend or erase some dark tones, just redo it with your pencil lightly.

- Use your pencil to fill any uneven light spots and for any uneven dark spots, just lift it with a kneaded eraser.

Cone

Step 1. Copy the shape below: You can trace it if you want or you can draw it by drawing a vertical line first and a short horizontal line. Then, use an ellipse template to draw the base and use ruler for the slope starting at the top of the vertical line going to one end of ellipse. Do the same to the other one.

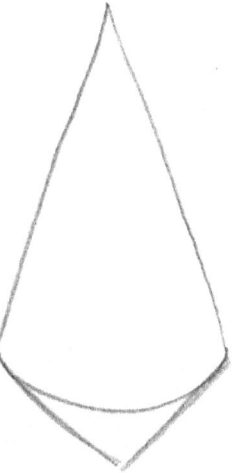

Step 2. Begin shading the cast shadow (6B).

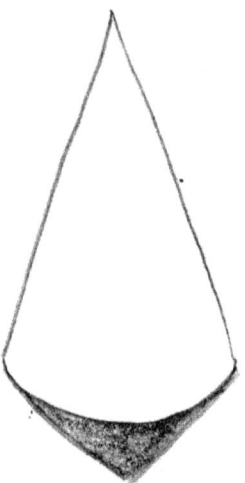

Step 3. Then, apply 2B to the shadow area, and also F to the inner circular area of the base. You can extend the F tone to the top, but do it lightly. Your stroke should be following the circular shape of the cone, but don't shade the right and left side near the slope, as that is where our highlights will be.

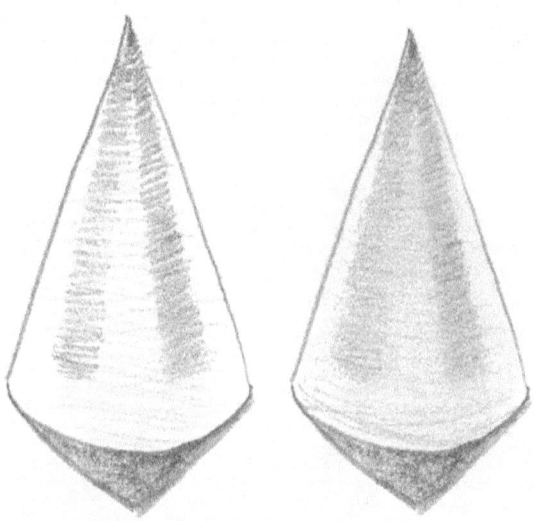

Step 4. Now for our midtones: On the line where we shaded the 2B, apply shading starting with HB lightly. Overlap the 2H tone and also the 4H, and do the same to the other side. Be careful to leave some space for our highlights for both sides.

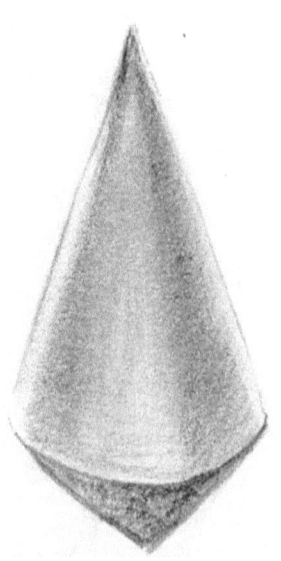

Step 5. Now let's blend everything one at a time, starting from F at the bottom. Start your stroke at the left moving to the right until you reach the top. Be careful when blending with 2B tone, not to smudge much. For 2B to midtones, slowly blend the 2B to HB, 2H and 4H, going to the outer side for both sides. Make sure highlights can be seen, so pull out the highlights using the kneaded eraser on that side. Also just between the 2B tones near the tip, erase so that it will look evident, then draw a line at the back of the cone.

Cube

Step 1. Copy the cube outline; you can trace or do it manually.

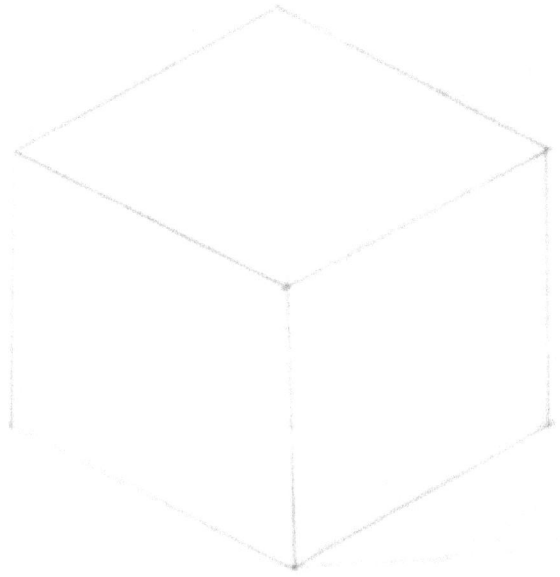

Step 2. Start shading with the cast shadow. In this example, the cast shadow on the right side is darker than the backside, and that's because the light source came from the left side.

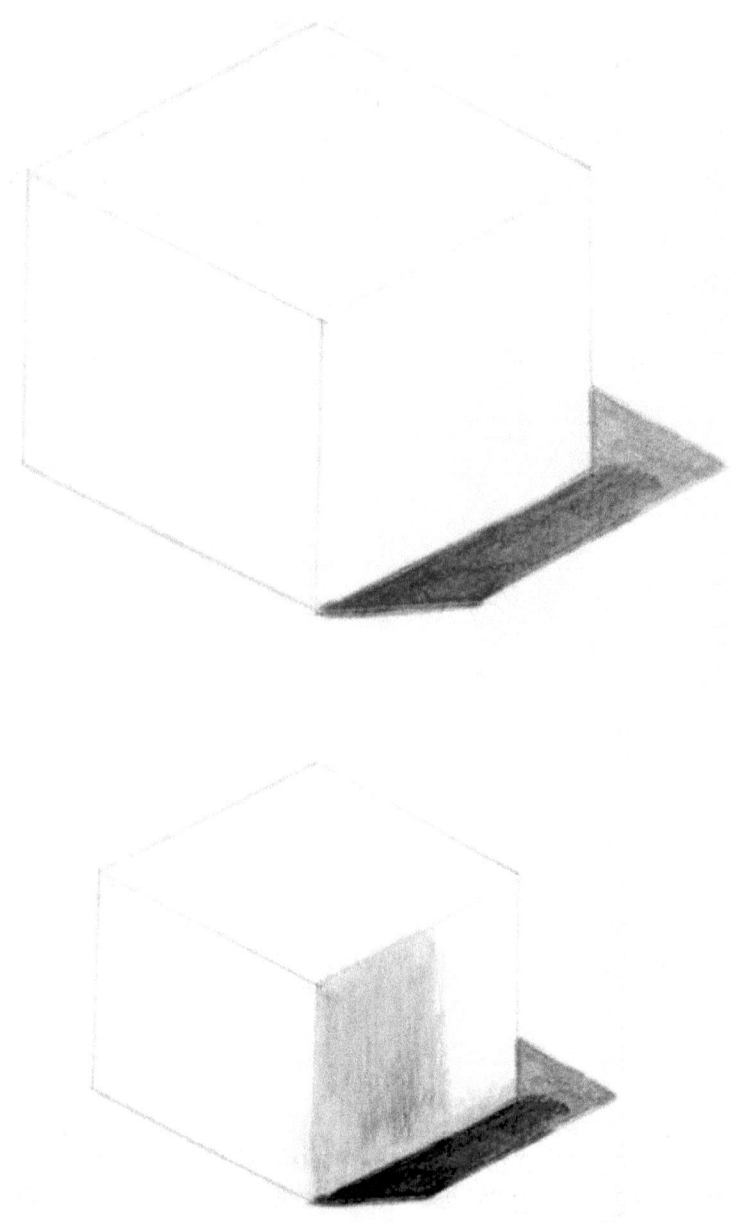

Step 3. Apply the shadow (2B), and also the reflected light (F) on the lower part of this side.

Step4. Add the midtones - HB, 2H and 4H, beside the shadow, and also shade a portion of HB below the front side.

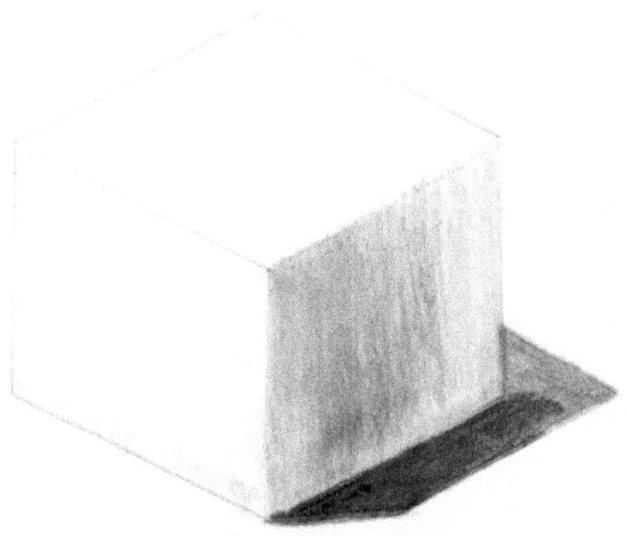

Step 5. Shade the front side with 2H until you fill half of this side, then switch to 4H and fill the rest.

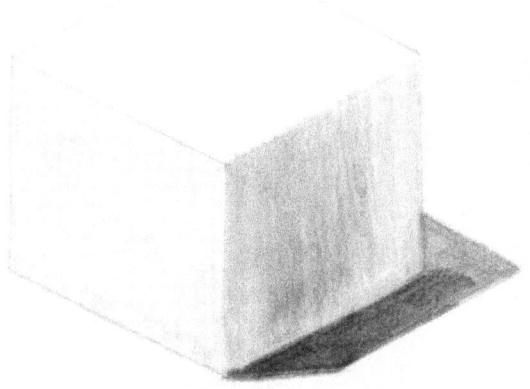

Step 6. Slightly shade a small tone on the right side at the top.

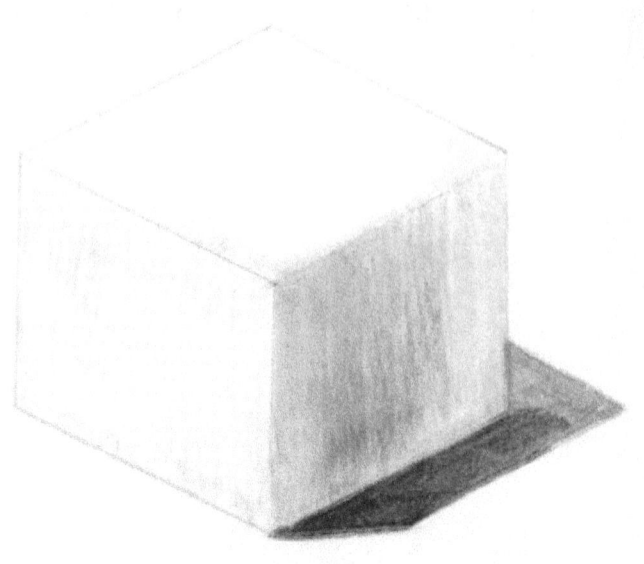

Step 7. Blend all respective sides accordingly with the smudge tool.

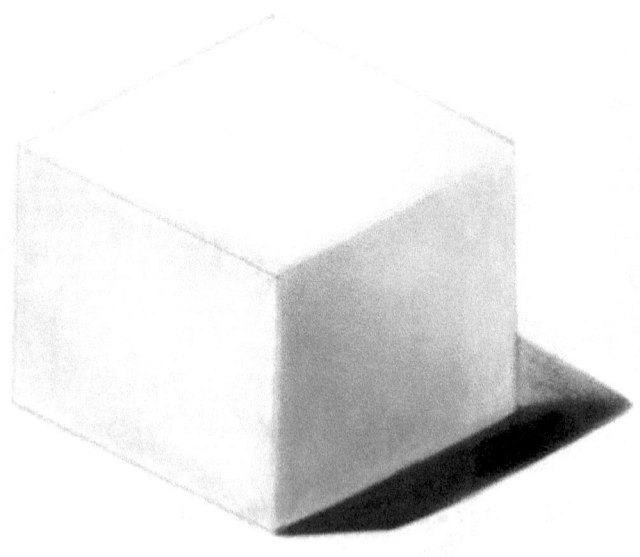

Cylinder

Step 1. Copy the outline or do it manually. The parts are composed of two ellipses and two vertical lines. The light is coming from left side, so the shadow would be at the back opposite the light source.

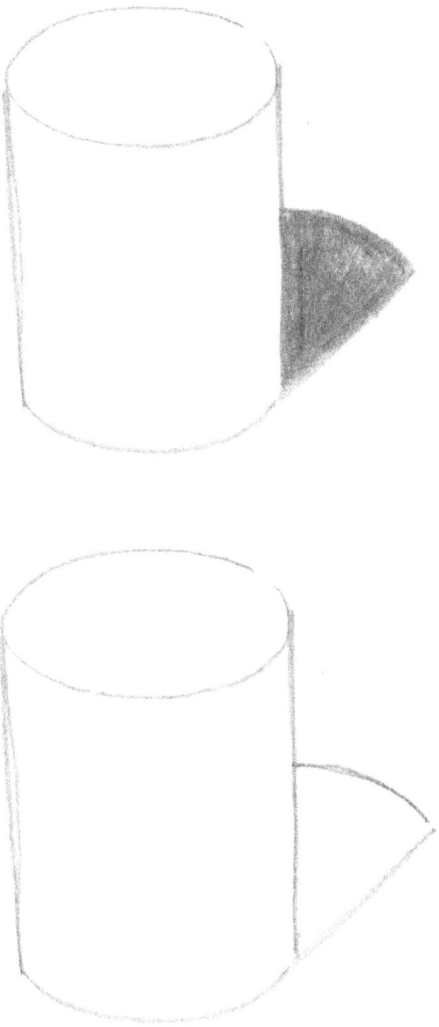

Step 2. Begin shading the cast shadow (6B) at the back.

Step 3. Next, apply the Shadow (2B), and take note of the roundness of the cylinder shape. There will be two shadows running vertically as seen in the illustration, so lightly apply F on the left side of the cylinder, vertically, beside the shadow.

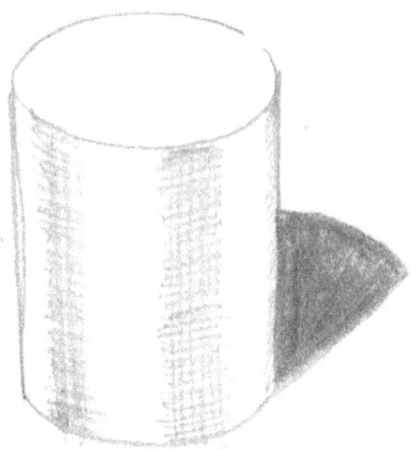

Step 4. Work your midtones, beside the two shadows, starting with HB, 2H and 4H. Also do it to the other side of each shadow, and apply these tones on the top of the cylinder.

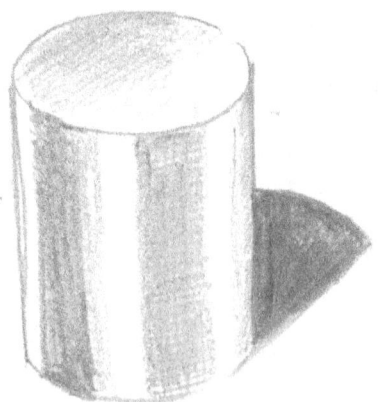

Step 5. Blend the cast shadow and shadows with the midtones (careful to leave empty space for the bands of highlights, we have three). Blend the top as well, and we're done.

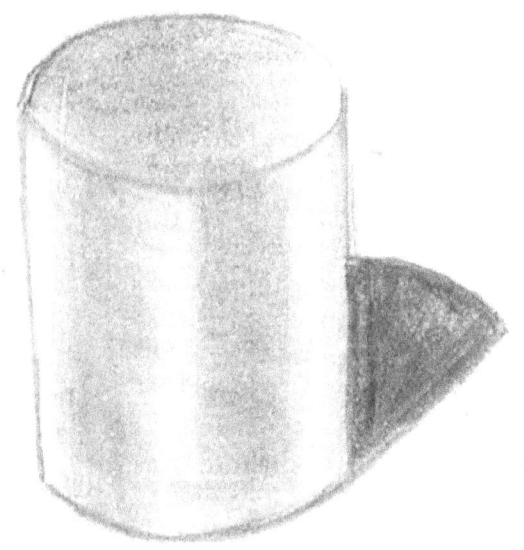

Layering

Smudging is good for softening the surface of your shading, but not all subjects look good or can be portrayed effectively with a soft appearance.

Sometimes you just want the inner surface of your subject to be grayish, but you don't want it to look soft. So the solution to this is to initiate the smudging process first, and then apply the secondary details afterwards. This method is a basic form of layering.

Layering simply means to know what should come first. But, when it comes to finalizing a drawing, layering becomes more significant since the proper order of applying shades and final details is crucial.

It is important to note that since smudging will blur the lines you made, some of the details of your subjects will blur as well.

Using a blending stump and kneaded eraser will really help you to avoid smearing important details accidentally, because using these tools will make it easy for you to reach the particular corners.

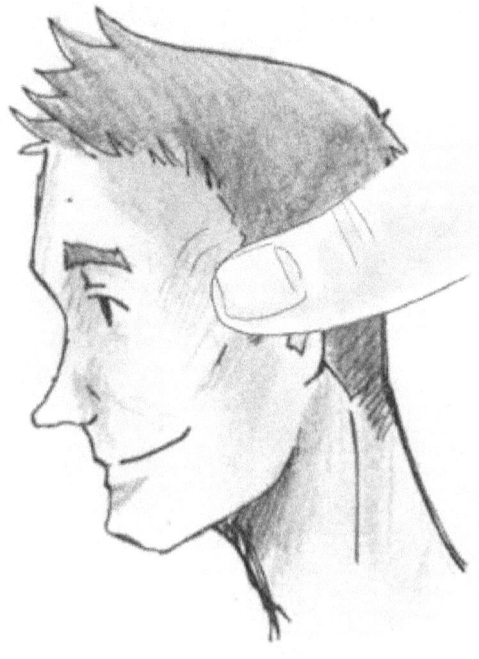

For using the smeared gray tone as a layer, which I mentioned before:

- initiate the smudging process

- get back to the smeared details and redefine the lines

- Give the texture, embellishment, or any particular markings as the last step.

Just simply change the order of your drawing method, that's all there is to it.

For layering the shade values

- Start with the general tone of the subject

- Apply the dark tones with pressure (enough to sync or fix it on the paper)

- Initiate the brightest tones and highlights with the kneaded eraser (use a regular eraser if you don't have one yet) using a light pressure.

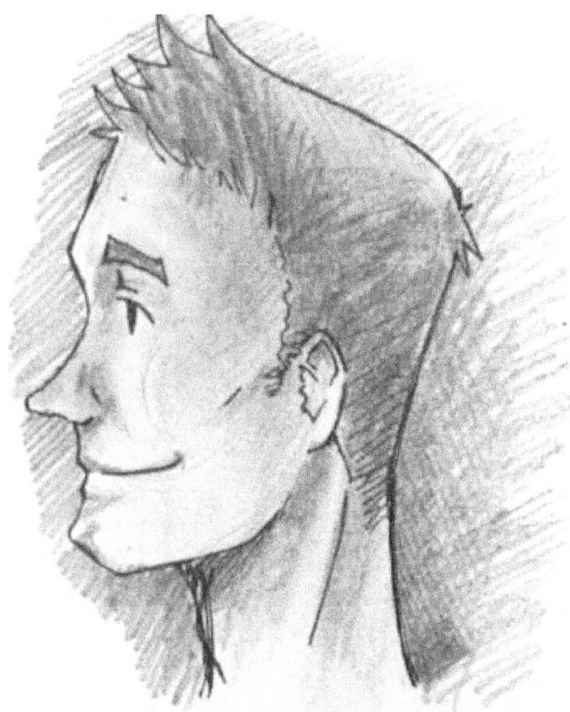

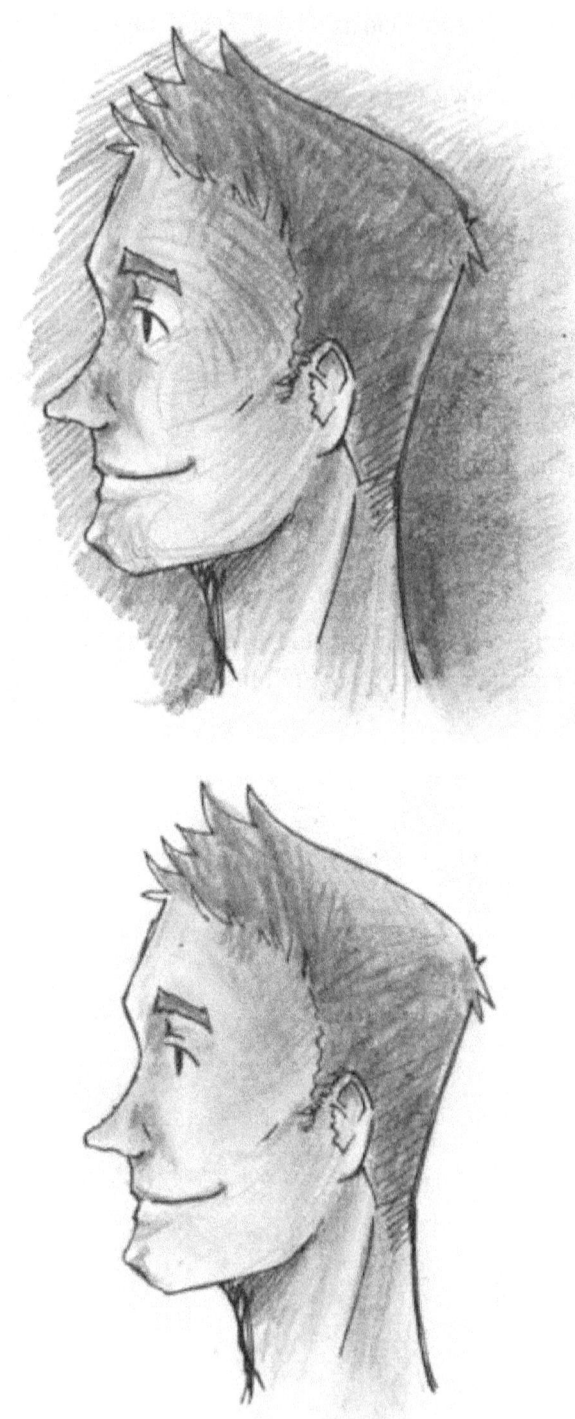

Design

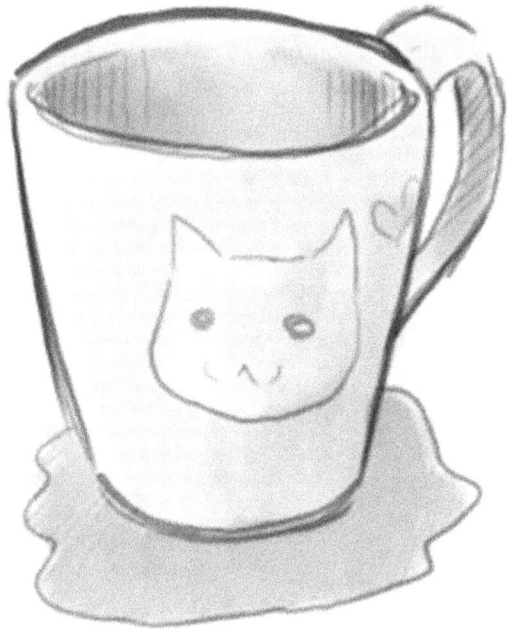

Details provide a better description to any subject of your drawing.

For example, rather than just drawing a plain serpentine dragon, give it some texture by drawing the most commonly seen thick armor scales. Embellishments give the subject more quality.

It can be a print design on a mug or a shirt, the furry hair of a cat, a tattoo or anything than can be rendered with lines or shade.

Fabrics

Details such as prints on fabrics should flow with the portrayed bends or folds, just like how it should appear naturally.

Observe the change in tension on the cloth such as if the tension goes inwards, outwards, pulled or loosely waved on one side. The details should flow along with the fabric and show the certain change in shape of the fabric's plane/surface.

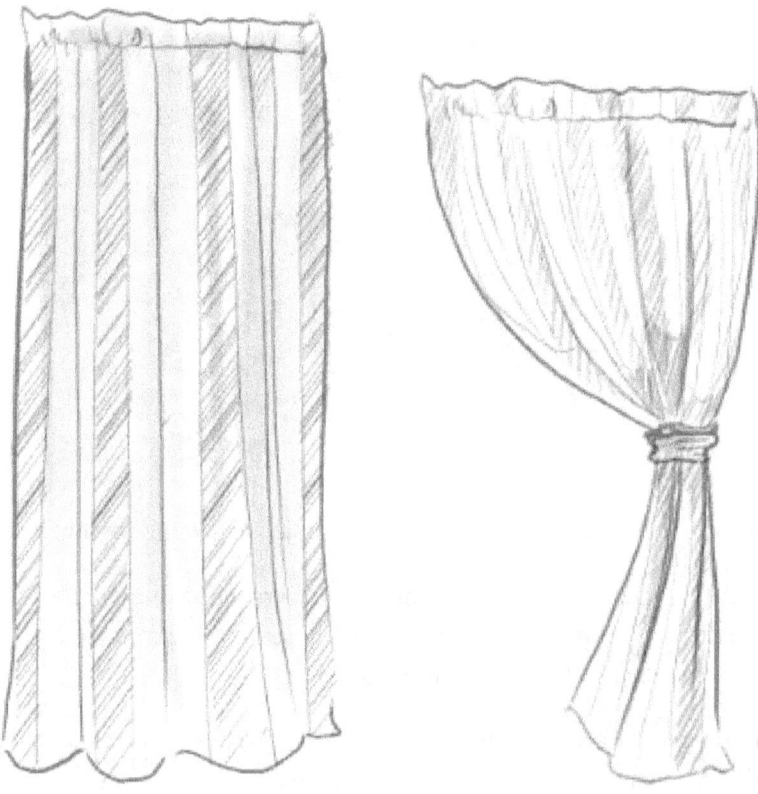

Textures and designs have more use, aside from giving additional description or personality to a subject. Some objects or a portion of a subject need more than just the main outline of its shape to describe dimension value.

Use textures and other embellishments to provide a better depiction of the subject's proportions. It might unintentionally appear flat if you don't present a good impression of its contour form (three-dimensional shape).

Here I have shown the effects of rendering and adding details to the subject---making it more realistic and textured.

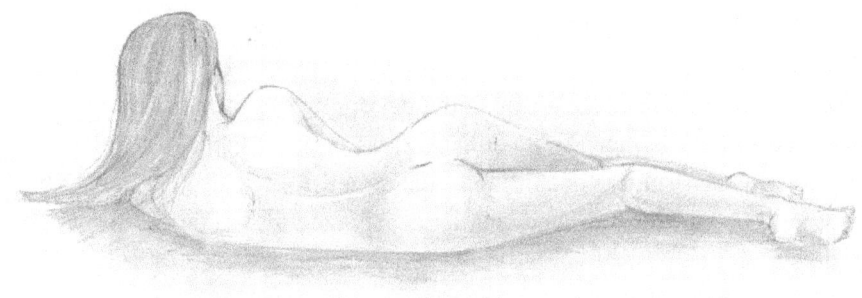

But, a detail or a design can also make the object look flat if it doesn't flow/bend accordingly with the object's contour form.

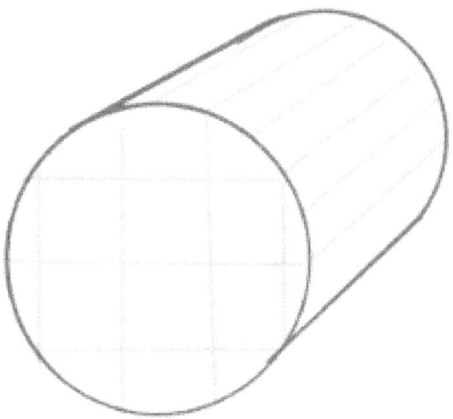

- To have a better idea on how a pattern should flow, imagine or mark a line that travels across the entire shape of the subject. If the pattern contains lines that are parallel to the main outline of your primary shape, then use it as a guide.

- The details, small shapes, or any embellishing marks should describe which portion of the main shape is nearer to the viewer's (you) point and which portion is positioned farther.

- You can use these lines as a reference if your pattern or design is aligned, and just add another set of lines from an opposite direction to make a grid and have a better reference. This is most useful for designs or markings with the same size.

The nearest point of the main shape should appear bigger, and considering that the size of the pattern is equal, the pattern or any form of detailing should also look bigger. As it bends with the contour shape of its plane, changing its own figure according to the dimensions of its plane, it should appear to become smaller and smaller as its plane moves farther from the nearest point.

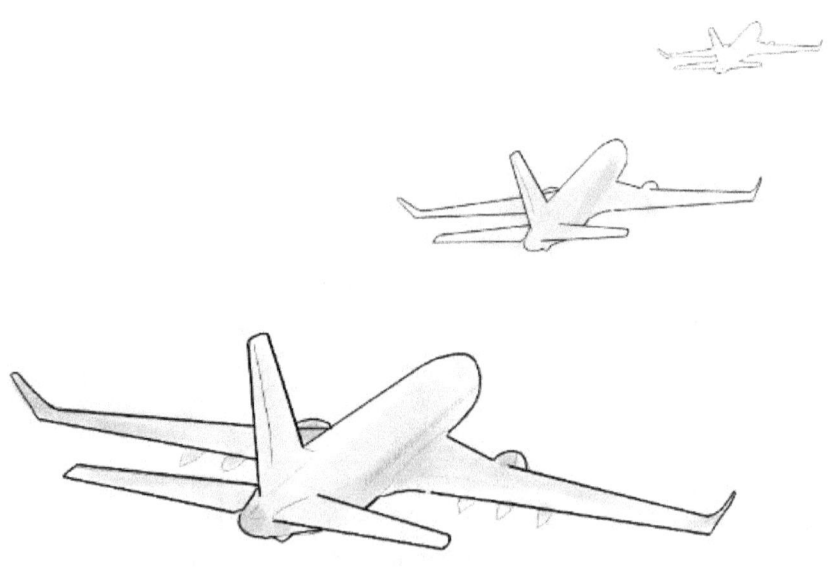

The manner of how the lines curve with the contour shape of the subject best describes the three dimensional value of its form.

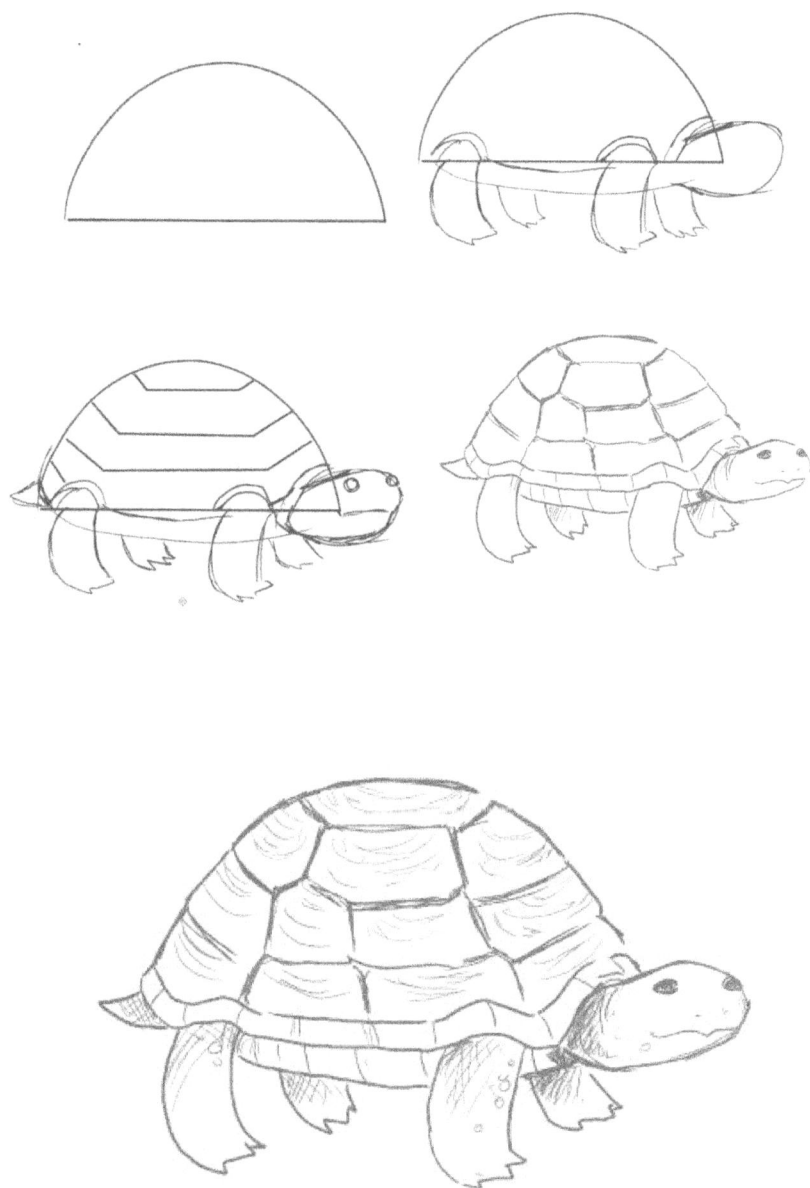

A spherical surface, such as the shell of the turtle, makes the center of its shape the nearest portion from the angle of its view. The details should have bigger figures or shapes that are largest at the center then gradually decreasing the size as it reaches the main outline.

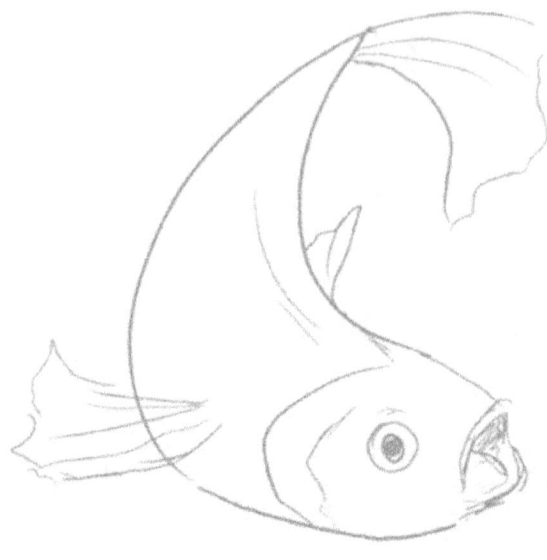

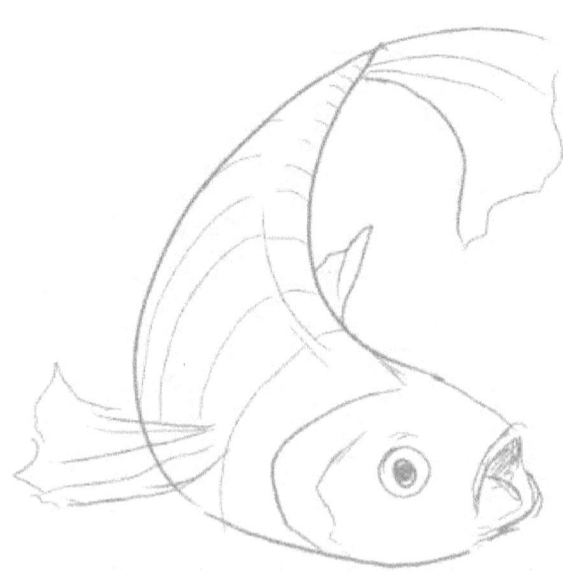

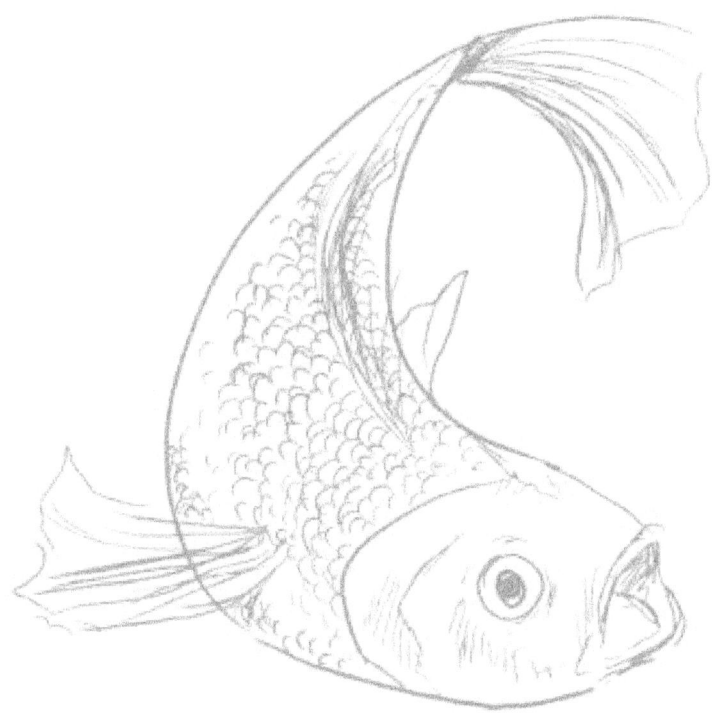

The main shape's viewpoint affects the appearance of details as well, aside from its natural dimension. The semi-cone shape of a fish would make its scales portray its position expressively. The scales should appear larger on the center of the cone and gradually get smaller as it reaches the outline, but the line sets should also appear smaller at the portion of the farther side of the body.

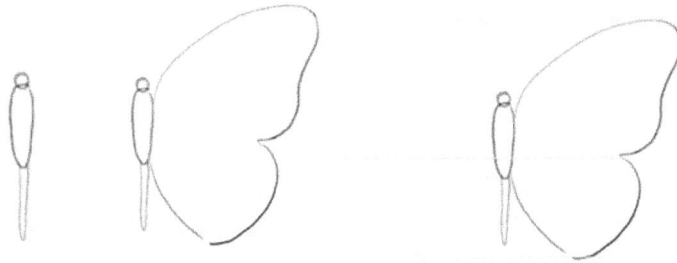

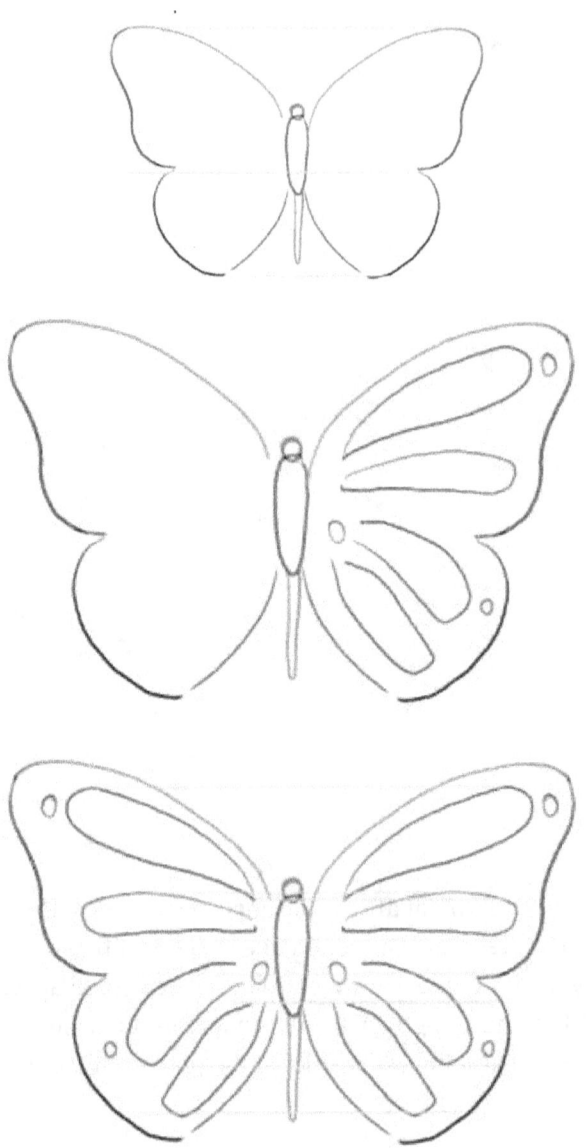

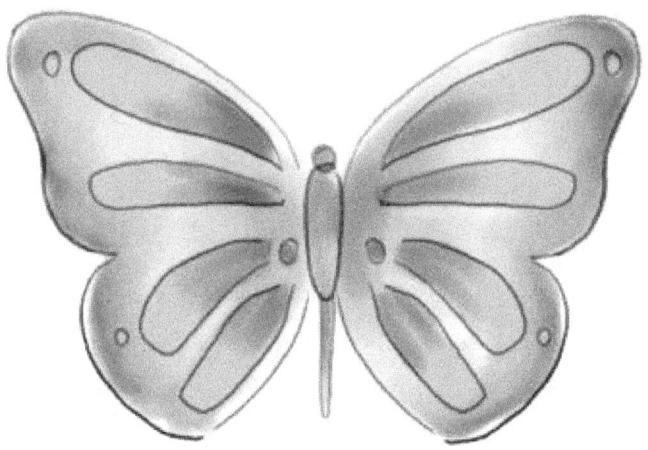

If your subject is flat and does not show a multidimensional angle or viewpoint then all you have to do is make the details aligned.

- Use reference lines to locate the edges of your details and indent them, just like forming a shape from connecting dots.

- Place indention marks to serve as a guide for the gaps, vertical lines, edges, and line curves.

Texture

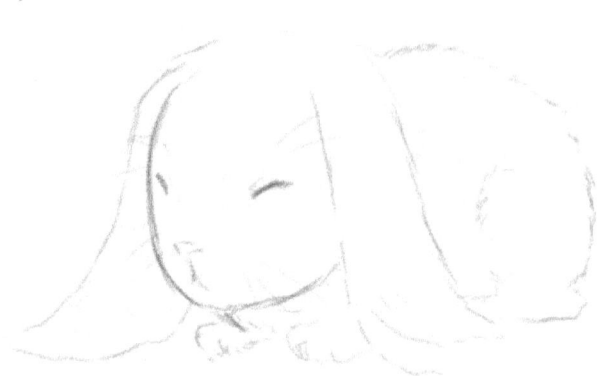

Textures are sometimes better portrayed in a different manner than embellishing the inner portion of your subject's main outline. Textures such as furs not only modify or embellish the figure within the outline, but also change the way an object is defined, by replacing or overlapping the outline itself.

- Short furs of a subject can be portrayed with short parallel diagonal lines.

Keep practicing until you no longer need to start with very basic shapes. Once you already know the primary form of your subject, then you can skip the shape-forming process and start with definitive silhouettes.

Long straight lines with different thickness and diminishing edges are fitted for portraying hairy textures such as a cat's fur.

- Show some direction on how the hair flows by following the basic shape of your subject.

- Start with thin lines first, then thicken it by using lines with more weight, but still end with fine diminishing edges (signatory lines) just as light, like those of the thin ones you first used.

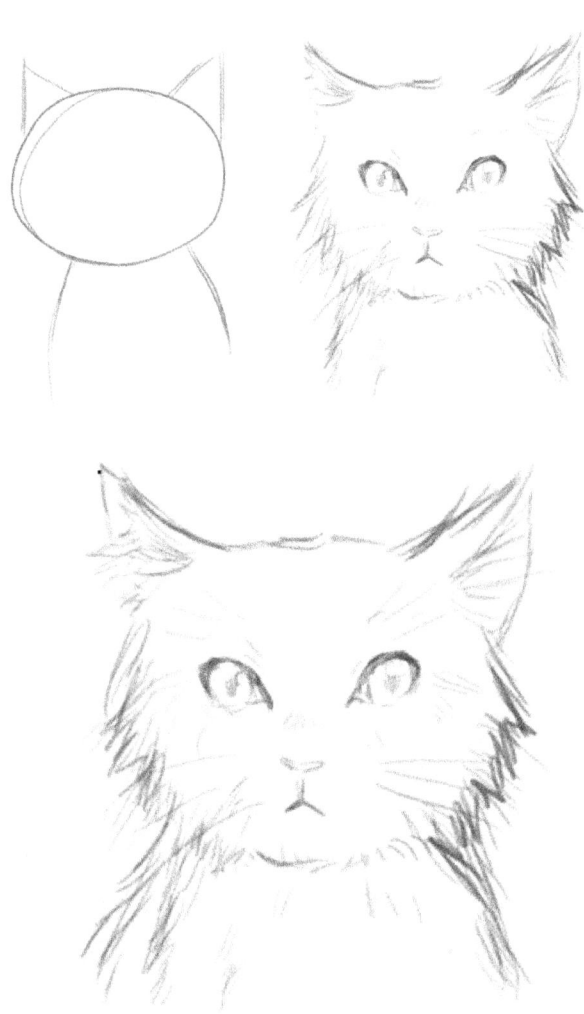

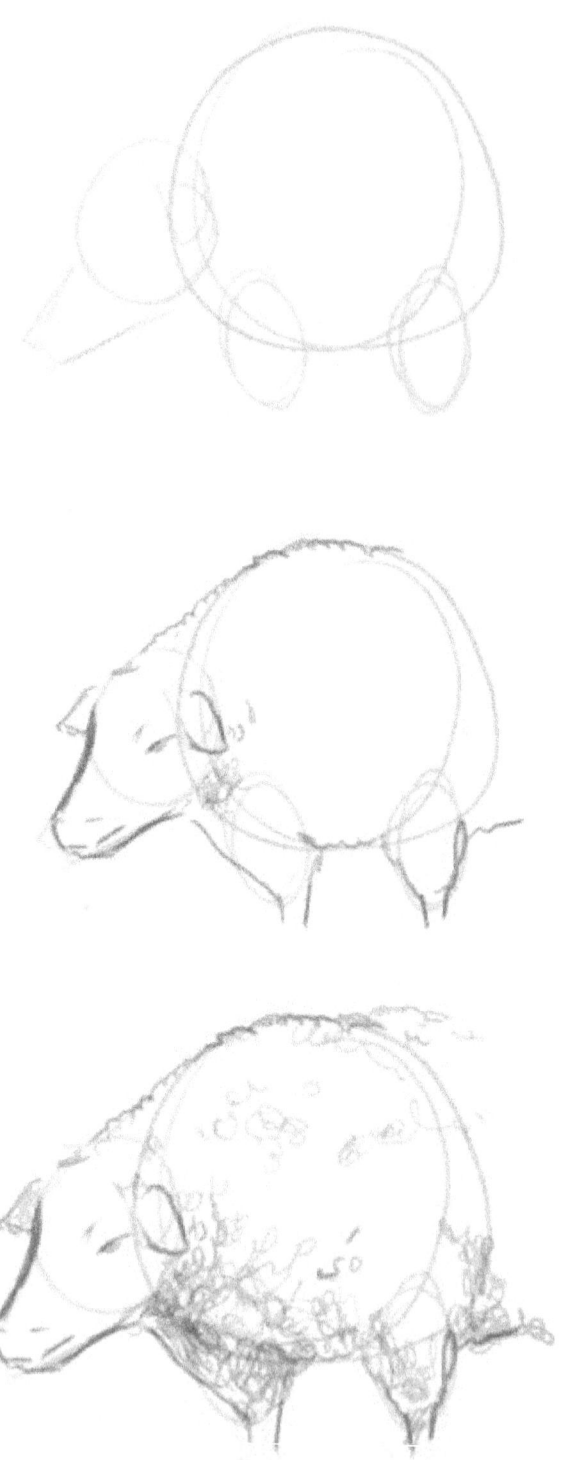

Fluffy textures, such as a sheep's thick fur, can be portrayed with scribbling lines.

- Use overlapping continuous circling lines when tracing the basic outline of your subject.

- Do not use any sharp line strokes to obtain a soft appearance.

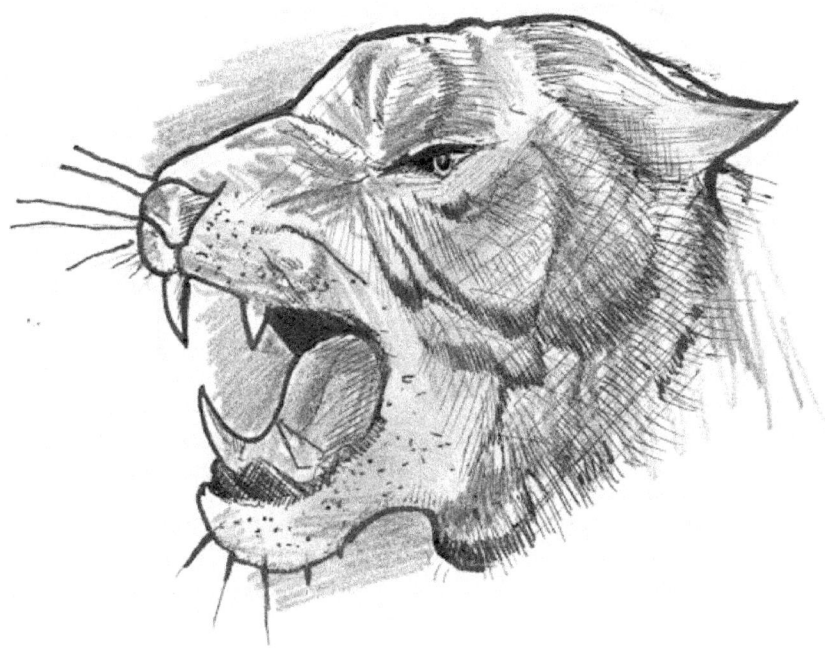

I hope you have enjoyed this lesson in Pencil Art for the Beginner. We have gone over all the basics, and have shown how to render as well as shade your drawings. Thank you for reading, and if you want to learn other techniques or expand your drawing abilities, check out our other series. Remember: Practice, Practice, Practice!

Author Bio

Being a young child, she has been inspired by the art of children story books her mother and father surrounded her with. From then on, she drew and drew---animals, plants, and things. She grew up in Indang, Cavite, Philippines where she also took up a course in BS Biology since she does not only took interest in drawing but also in Sciences. The place they had in Indang is rich in flora. They had gardens which yielded vegetables and flowers. To live in such a wonderful place inspired her to learn painting, too. You can see the young Harriet draw under the shade of the tree or next to their small and simple garden.

Due to financial problems, she was not able to take Fine Arts as course but she continued studying arts. She was known in the school as an artist good in drawing anime characters and making projects for Drafts. In college, she studied in Cavite State University and took up BS Biology where she excelled in Chemistry, Biology and Mathematics. She also applied in Gazette—the Official Student Publication unit of the university where she learned cartooning and using Photoshop. She also started working as an artist while studying.

In the year 2013, her family moved to Pampanga, Philippines; and so, she transferred to a different school, Angeles University Foundation, where she is currently continuing her studies in BS Biology.

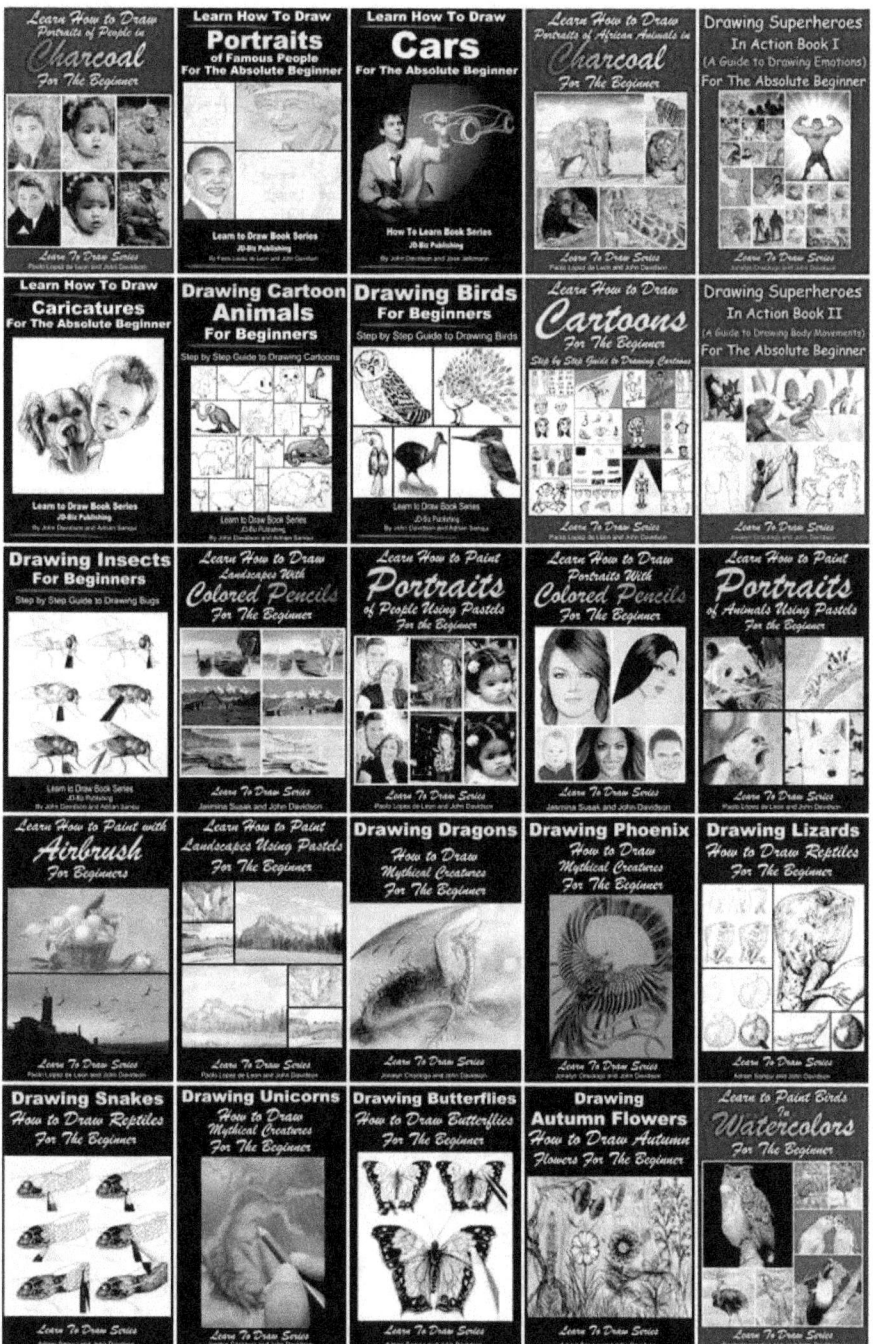

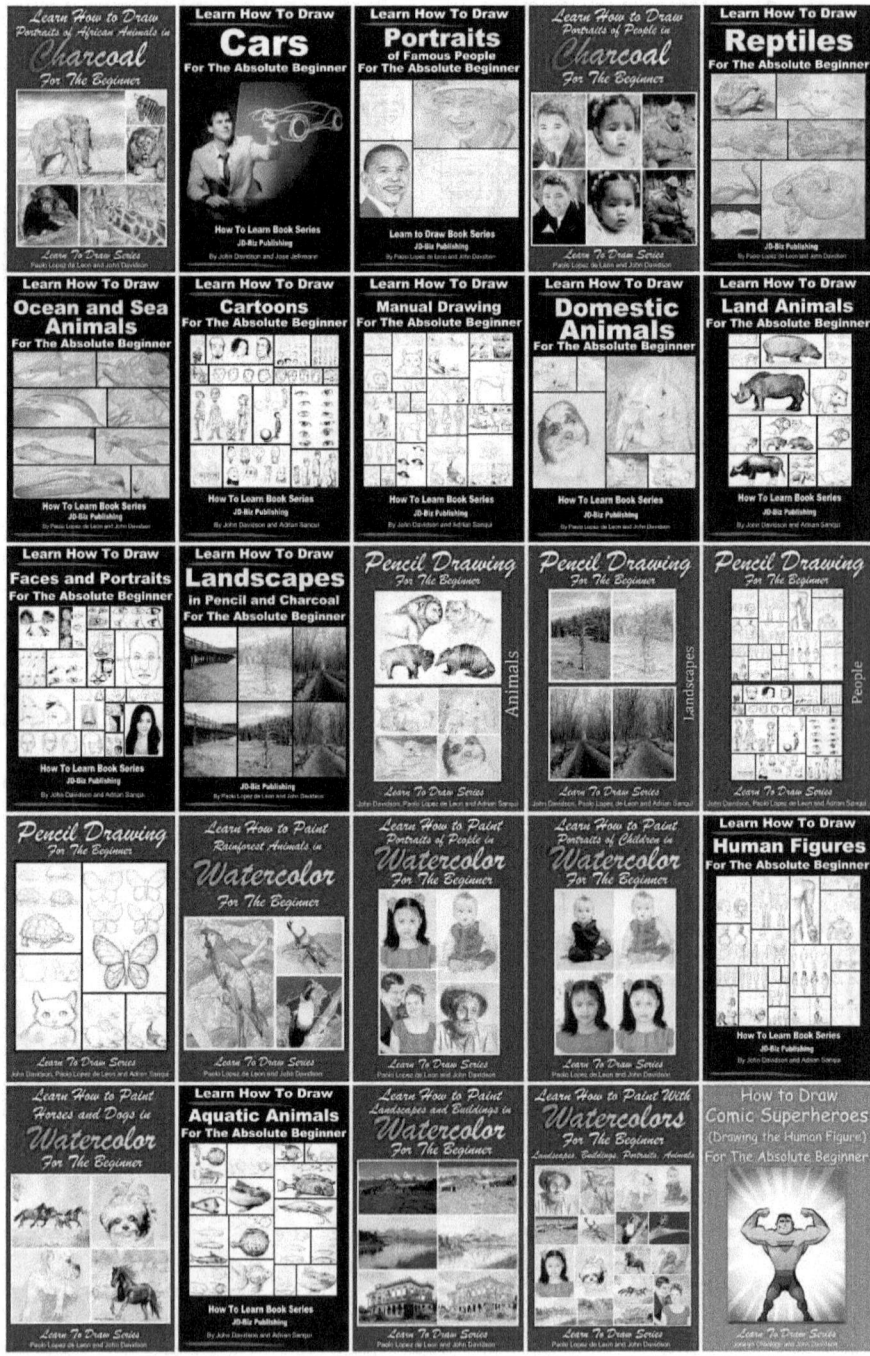

Publisher

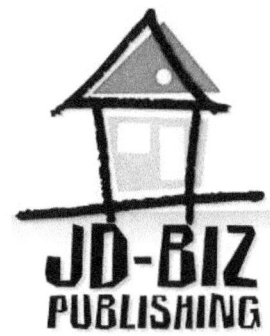

JD-Biz Corp

P O Box 374

Mendon, Utah 84325

http://www.jd-biz.com/

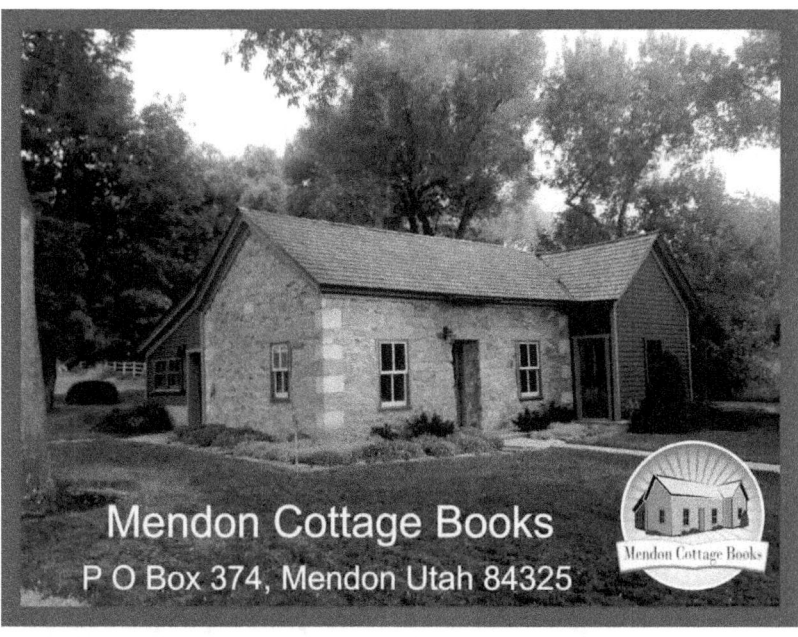

www.ingramcontent.com/pod-product-compliance
Lightning Source LLC
Chambersburg PA
CBHW070930180526
45168CB00003B/1014